PRE
D

CW00344976

Volume

1st Edition

Iain Dobson &
Neil Webster

metro

ISBN 0-947773-34-7

1

NOTES

PRESERVATION DATAFILE is produced as a budget priced handy pocket size guide to former BR locomotives & multiple units now in preservation or industrial use. This volume covers Diesel & Electric Vehicles, whilst Volume 2 covers Steam Vehicles.

INDEX

PART ONE - LOCOMOTIVES
 1.1 Locomotives classified under the TOPS system | 6
 1.2 Locomotives not classified under the TOPS system | 31
 1.3 Locomotives withdrawn prior to 1st January 1948 | 34
 1.4 Former War Department Locomotives | 37
 1.5 Manufacturers prototypes not taken into BR stock | 37

PART TWO - DIESEL MULTIPLE UNITS
 2.1 "First Generation" vehicles | 38
 2.2 "Second Generation" vehicles | 55
 2.3 Advanced Passenger Train vehicles | 57
 2.4 Former Great Western Railway vehicles | 58

PART THREE - ELECTRIC MULTIPLE UNITS
 3.1 Post-nationalisation vehicles | 59
 3.2 Former LMS & constituent companies' vehicles | 62
 3.3 Former Southern Railway vehicles | 64
 3.4 Former LNER & constituent companies' vehicles | 66
 3.5 Former Pullman Car Company vehicles | 67

LIST OF LOCOMOTIVE NAMES | 68
LIST OF INDUSTRIAL USERS | 70
LIST OF PRESERVATION SITES | 74

LAYOUT OF INFORMATION

All Sections
Technical data relates to as built condition and takes no account of any subsequent modifications.

Section 1.1
Locomotives are arranged in class number order. The tabular details are arranged in columns as shown in the following example:

02003   D2853   06.75   LCP Fuels, Brierley Hill   SU

Column 1 is the TOPS number. Where more than one number has been carried
         over the years by a particular locomotive, the number carried carried for
         the greatest length of time is shown, with details of other numbers
         carried given as notes.
Column 2 is the 1957 series number (where applicable).
Column 3 is the withdrawal date from BR service (excluding periods in use for
         other than traction purposes.
Column 4 is the current location (or intended location of recently purchased
         vehicles).
Column 5 is the current status (see status code list below).

Sections 1.2-1.5
Locomotives are arranged in number order, 1948 series numbers preceding 1957
numbers and Departmental numbers. The tabular details are arranged in columns
as shown in the following example:

18000   02.60   UIC ORE Testing Station, Vienna, Austria   IE

Column 1 is the locomotive number. Where more than one number has been
         carried by a particular locomotive, other numbers are given as notes.
Column 2 is the withdrawal date from BR or WD service.
Column 3 is the current location.
Column 4 is the current status (see status code list below).

Sections 2.1-2.4
Vehicles are arranged in numerical order of final number carried on BR. The tabular
details are arranged in columns as shown in the following example:

53019   50019   06.92   Midland Railway Centre   OP

Column 1 is the final number carried on BR.
Column 2 is the previous number carried on BR (where applicable).
Column 3 is the withdrawal date from BR service.
Column 4 is the current location (or intended location of recently purchased
         vehicles).
Column 5 is the current status (see status code list below).

Sections 3.1-3.5
Vehicles are arranged in order of classes, then order of vehicle numbers. The
tabular details are arranged in columns as shown in the following example:

29289   DTSO   03.85   Shore Road Museum, Birkenhead   CE

Column 1 is the vehicle number.

Column 2 is the type of vehicle within a set (as applicable) or (in section 3.5) the vehicle name.

Column 3 is the withdrawal date from BR service.

Column 4 is the current location (or intended location of recently purchased vehicles).

Column 5 is the current status (see status code list below).

STATUS CODES

CC	In use as a Camping Coach.
CE	Complete Museum Exhibit.
EX	Exported, current fate unknown.
IE	Incomplete Museum Exhibit.
ML	Approved for main line running on British Rail.
OP	Operational, but not approved for main line running.
OH	Operational as hauled stock only (multiple unit vehicles).
SB	Stored on BR.
SS	Stored in a serviceable condition.
SU	Stored in an unserviceable condition.
UR	Undergoing repairs.

Where the status column in blank, the current status of the vehicle is not known.

OTHER ABBREVIATIONS

Other abbreviations used in this book are as follows:

ac	Alternating current.
BE	Battery Electric.
BR	British Railways.
dc	Direct current.
DE	Diesel-electric.
DH	Diesel-hydraulic.
DM	Diesel-mechanical.
DMBC	Driving Motor Brake Composite.
DMBS	Driving Motor Brake Second.
DMBSL	Driving Motor Brake Second with lavatory.
DMBT	Driving Motor Brake Third.
DMCL	Driving Motor Composite with lavatory.
DMPMV	Driving Motor Parcels & Miscellaneous Van.
DMS	Driving Motor Second.
DML	Driving Motor Second with lavatory.
DTBS	Driving Trailer Brake Second.
DTCL	Driving Trailer Composite with lavatory.

DTS	Driving Trailer Second.
ED	Third Rail Electric/Diesel-electric.
GTE	Gas Turbine-electric.
GWR	Great Western Railway.
Hz	Hertz.
kV	Kilovolts.
kW	Kilowatts.
LMS	London Midland & Scottish Railway.
LNER	London & North Eastern Railway.
M	Motor coach.
m.	Metres.
mm.	Millimetres.
mph	Miles per hour.
OE	Overhead Electric.
PC	Power Car.
RE	Third Rail Electric.
rpm	Revolutions per minute.
SR	Southern Railway.
t	tons.
TBF	Trailer Brake First with lavatory.
TBFKL	Trailer Brake First (Corridor) with lavatory.
TBS	Trailer Brake Second.
TBSL	Trailer Brake Second with lavatory.
TC	Trailer Composite. (Trailer Car - APT-E only).
TCL	Trailer Composite with lavatory.
TFK	Trailer First (Corridor).
TFLK	Trailer First (Corridor) with lavatory.
TS	Trailer Second.
TSK	Trailer Second (Corridor).
TSL	Trailer Second with lavatory.
TSLRB	Trailer Second Miniature Buffet with lavatory.
v.	Volts.

ACKNOWLEDGEMENTS

Our grateful thanks to all who have helped in the compilation of this book. In particular special thanks are due to Simon Bennett, Trevor Green, Andrew Mitchell, David Russell, Craig Ryan, John Sandham, Ted Slee and Robert Whitehead.

COVER PHOTOGRAPHS

Front: D7672 at M.C. Metal Processing for asbestos removal.   (Dave Campbell)

Back: E5001 at Chart Leacon depot.

(Neil Webster)

CLASS 01   0-6-0 DM

Built: 1956 by Andrew Barclay, Kilmarnock.
Engine: Gardner 6L3 of 114 kW at 1200 rpm.
Length over buffers: 7.214 m.   **Weight:** 25.05 t.
Extreme width: 2.578 m.   **Wheel Diameter:** 965 mm.
Extreme height: 3.616 m.   **Maximum Permitted Speed:** 14.25 mph
Original Numbers: 11503 & 11506 respectively.

	D2953	06.66	South Yorkshire Railway	OP
	D2956	05.66	East Lancashire Railway	SU

CLASS 02   0-4-0 DH

Built: 1960-61 by Yorkshire Engine Company, Sheffield.
Engine: Rolls Royce C6NFL Series 176 of 126 kW at 1800 rpm.
Length over buffers: 6.702 m.   **Weight:** 28.15 t.
Extreme width: 2.591 m.   **Wheel Diameter:** 1067 mm.
Extreme height: 3.486 m.   **Maximum Permitted Speed:** 19.5 mph

02003	D2853	06.75	LCP Fuels, Brierley Hill	SU
	D2854	02.70	South Yorkshire Railway	OP
	D2857	04.71	Birds Commercial Metals, Long Marston	SU
	D2858	02.70	Butterley Engineering Co, Ripley	OP
	D2860	12.70	National Railway Museum	OP
	D2866	02.70	Caledonian Railway	OP
	D2867	09.70	Redland Roadstone, Barrow on Soar	OP
	D2868	12.69	LCP Fuels, Brierley Hill	SU

CLASS 03   0-6-0 DM

Built: 1958-62 by BR at Swindon or Doncaster Works.
Engine: Gardner 8L3 of 152 kW at 1200 rpm.
Length over buffers: 7.925 m.   **Weight:** 30.20 t.
Extreme width: 2.591 m.   **Wheel Diameter:** 1092 mm.
Extreme height: 3.720 m.   **Maximum Permitted Speed:** 28 5 mph

Original Numbers: 03371 was originally Departmental No. 92.

Note: † expected to move to the South Yorkshire Railway during 1993.

03018	D2018	11.75	Ferrous Fragmentisers, Willesden	OP
	D2019	07.71	ISA, Ospitaletto, Italy	OP
03020	D2020	12.75	Mayer Parry, Snailwell	OP
03022	D2022	11.82	Swindon & Cricklade Railway	OP
	D2023	07.71	Kent & East Sussex Steam Railway	UR
	D2024	07.71	Kent & East Sussex Steam Railway	UR
03027	D2027	01.76	South Yorkshire Railway	SU
	D2032	08.71	ISA, Ospitaletto, Italy	OP
	D2033	12.71	Siderurgica, Montirone, Italy	SU
	D2036	12.71	Siderurgica, Montirone, Italy	OP
03037	D2037	09.76	BCOE, Oxcroft Disposal Point	OP
	D2041	02.70	Colne Valley Railway	OP
	D2046	10.71	Gulf Oil, Waterston	OP
	D2051	10.71	Ford Motor Company, Dagenham	OP
03059	D2059	07.87	Isle of Wight Steam Railway	OP
03062	D2062	12.80	Dean Forest Railway	UR
03063	D2063	11.87	Colne Valley Railway	OP
03066	D2066	01.88	South Yorkshire Railway	OP
03069	D2069	12.83	Gloucestershire Warwickshire Railway	OP
	D2070	11.71	Private site in Derbyshire	UR
03072	D2072	03.81	Lakeside & Haverthwaite Railway	OP
03073	D2073	03.89	The Railway Age, Crewe	OP
03078	D2078	01.88	North Tyneside Steam Railway	OP
03081	D2081	12.80	Charleroi, Belgium	EX
03084	D2084	07.87	Private site in Derbyshire	UR
03089	D2089	11.87	Mangapps Farm Railway Museum	OP
03090	D2090	07.76	National Railway Museum	OP
03094	D2094	01.88	South Yorkshire Railway	OP
03099	D2099	02.76	South Yorkshire Railway	UR
03112	D2112	07.87	Nene Valley Railway	OP
03113	D2113	08.75	Heritage & Maritime Museum, Milford Haven	IE
	D2117	10.71	Lakeside & Haverthwaite Railway	OP
	D2118	06.72	Costain Dow-Mac, Lenwade	SS
03119	D2119	02.86	Dean Forest Railway	OP
03120	D2120	02.86	Fawley Hill Railway	OP
03128	D2128	07.76	Peak Rail PLC	UR
	D2133	07.69	Courtaulds, Bridgwater	OP
03134	D2134	07.76	Stoomcentrum, Maldegem, Belgium †	UR
	D2138	05.69	Midland Railway Centre	OP
	D2139	05.68	South Yorkshire Railway	OP
03141	D2141	07.85	J.M. DeMulder, Shilton	SU
03144	D2144	02.86	Ministry of Defence, Long Marston	OP

03145	D2145	07.85	J.M. DeMulder, Shilton	SU
	D2148	11.72	Southport Railway Centre	OP
	D2150	11.72	British Salt, Middlewich	OP
03152	D2152	10.83	Swindon & Cricklade Railway	OP
03158	D2158	07.87	Private site in Derbyshire	UR
03162	D2162	03.89	Llangollen Railway	OP
03170	D2170	03.89	Otis Euro-Transrail, Salford	OP
	D2178	09.69	Caerphilly Railway Centre	OP
03180	D2180	03.84	South Yorkshire Railway	SU
	D2182	05.68	Gloucestershire Warwickshire Railway	UR
	D2184	12.68	Colne Valley Railway	OP
03189	D2189	03.86	Southport Railway Centre	UR
	D2192	01.69	Paignton & Dartmouth Steam Railway	OP
03196	D2196	06.83	Steamtown Railway Centre	OP
03197	D2197	07.87	South Yorkshire Railway	UR
	D2199	06.72	South Yorkshire Railway	OP
03371	D2371	11.87	Rowden Mill Station Museum	OP
	D2381	06.72	Steamtown Railway Centre	OP
03399	D2399	07.87	Mangapps Farm Railway Museum	OP

CLASS 04   0-6-0 DM

Built: 1952-61 by English Electric, Vulcan Foundry, Newton-le-Willows or Robert Stephenson & Hawthorn, Darlington.
Engine: Gardner 8L3 of 152 kW at 1200 rpm.
Length over buffers: 7.931 m.   **Weight:** 30.25 t.
Extreme width: 2.591 m.   **Wheel Diameter:** 1092 (*991,†1067)mm
Extreme height: 3.693 m.
Maximum Permitted Speed: 27.8 (*25.8) mph
Original Numbers: 11103 (D2203), 11106 (D2205), 11108 (D2207), 11122 (D2216), 11135 (D2229), 11151 (D2232), 11215 (D2245), 11216 (D2246).

	D2203*	12.67	Embsay Steam Railway	OP
	D2205*	07.69	West Somerset Railway	OP
	D2207*	12.67	North Yorkshire Moors Railway	OP
	D2216†	05.71	ISA, Ospitaletto, Italy	OP
	D2229†	12.69	South Yorkshire Railway	OP
	D2232†	03.68	Rome, Italy	SU
	D2245†	12.68	Battlefield Steam Railway	UR
	D2246†	07.68	British Coal, West Drayton	OP
	D2267	12.69	Ford Motor Company, Dagenham	OP
	D2271	10.69	West Somerset Railway	OP
	D2272	10.70	British Fuels, Blackburn	OP
	D2279	05.71	East Anglian Railway Museum	OP
	D2280	03.71	Ford Motor Company, Dagenham	SU

D2284	04.71	South Yorkshire Railway	SU
D2295	04.71	Acciaierie, Lonato, Italy	OP
D2298	12.68	Buckinghamshire Railway Centre	OP
D2302	06.69	Potter Group, Ely	OP
D2310	01.69	Southern Depot Company, Tolworth	
D2324	07.68	Redland Roadstone, Barrow on Soar	OP
D2325	07.68	Mangapps Farm Railway Museum	OP
D2334	07.68	South Yorkshire Railway	OP
D2337	07.68	South Yorkshire Railway	SU

CLASS 05   0-6-0 DM

Built: 1956-60 by Hunslet Engine Company, Leeds.
Engine: Gardner 8L3 of 152 kW at 1200 rpm.
Length over buffers: 7.722 m.   **Weight:** 30.90 t.
Extreme width: 2.515 m.   **Wheel Diameter:** 1143 (* 1016) mm.
Extreme height: 3.353 m.   **Maximum Permitted Speed:** 17.8 mph
Original Number: D2554 was originally 11140.
Subsequent Number: 05001 later became 97803 in Departmental Service.

05001	D2554*	09.83	Isle of Wight Steam Railway	OP
	D2578	06.67	Bulmer Railway Centre	OP
	D2587	12.67	East Lancashire Railway	OP
	D2595	06.68	Southport Railway Centre	OP

CLASS 06   0-4-0 DM

Built: 1959 by Andrew Barclay, Kilmarnock.
Engine: Gardner 8L3 of 152 kW at 1200 rpm.
Length over buffers: 7.899 m.   **Weight:** 36.75 t.
Extreme width: 2.565 m.   **Wheel Diameter:** 1092 mm.
Extreme height: 3.612 m.   **Maximum Permitted Speed:** 22.8 mph
Subsequent Number: 97804 in Departmental Service.

06003	D2420	09.84	South Yorkshire Railway	OP

CLASS 07   0-6-0 DE

Built: 1962 by Ruston & Hornsby, Lincoln.
Engine: Paxman 6RPHL Mk. III of 204 kW at 1360 rpm.
Length over buffers: 8.166 m.   **Weight:** 42.25 t.
Extreme width: 2.591 m.   **Wheel Diameter:** 1067 mm.
Extreme height: 3.912 m.   **Maximum Permitted Speed:** 20 mph.

07001	D2985	07.77	South Yorkshire Railway	OP
07005	D2989	07.77	ICI, Wilton	SU

	D2991	05.73	BRML, Eastleigh	OP
07010	D2994	10.76	West Somerset Railway	OP
07011	D2995	07.77	ICI, Wilton	OP
07012	D2996	07.77	South Yorkshire Railway	SU
07013	D2997	07.77	Dow Chemicals, Kings Lynn	OP

CLASS 08   0-6-0 DE

Built: 1952-61 by BR at Derby Locomotive, Darlington, Crewe or Horwich Works.
Engine: English Electric 6KT of 297 kW at 680 rpm.
Length over buffers: 8.915 m.   **Weight:** 49.00 (* 48.60) t.
Extreme width: 2.915 m.   **Wheel Diameter:** 1372 mm.
Extreme height: 3.877 m.   **Maximum Permitted Speed:** 20 mph.
Original Numbers: D3000-D3336/66 were originally 13000-13336/66 in sequence.

	D3000	07.72	South Yorkshire Railway	UR
	D3002	07.72	Plym Valley Railway	UR
	D3014	10.72	Paignton & Dartmouth Railway	OP
08011	D3018	12.91	Chinnor & Princes Risborough Railway	OP
	D3019	06.73	South Yorkshire Railway	SU
08015	D3022	09.80	Severn Valley Railway	OP
08016	D3023	05.80	South Yorkshire Railway	OP
08021	D3029	04.86	Birmingham Railway Museum	OP
08022	D3030	03.86	Arthur Guinness, Park Royal	OP
08032	D3044	08.74	Foster Yeoman, Merehead	
	D3047	07.73	LAMCO Mining Company, Liberia	EX
08046	D3059	05.80	Caledonian Railway	OP
08054	D3067	12.80	Tilcon, Grassington	OP
08060	D3074	06.84	Arthur Guinness, Park Royal	OP
08064	D3079	12.84	National Railway Museum	UR
	D3092*	10.72	LAMCO Mining Company, Liberia	EX
	D3094*	10.72	LAMCO Mining Company, Liberia	EX
	D3098*	10.72	LAMCO Mining Company, Liberia	EX
	D3100*	10.72	LAMCO Mining Company, Liberia	EX
	D3101*	05.72	Great Central Railway	UR
08077	D3102	11.77	RFS Locomotives (For Hire)	OP
08102	D3167	03.88	Lincoln Central Station	IE
08108	D3174	07.84	East Kent Light Railway	OP
08113	D3179	03.84	PD Fuels, Gwaun-Cae-Gurwen DP	OP
08114	D3180	11.83	Great Central Railway	OP
08123	D3190	03.84	Cholsey & Wallingford Railway	OP
08133	D3201	09.80	Sheerness Steel Company, Sheerness	SS
08157	D3225	04.77	Independent Sea Terminals, Swale	OP
08164	D3232	03.86	RFS Locomotives (For Hire)	OP
08168	D3236	03.88	ABB Transportation, York	OP

	D3255	12.72	Brighton Railway Museum	UR
	D3261	12.72	Brighton Railway Museum	SU
08195	D3265	09.83	Llangollen Railway	OP
08202	D3272	04.89	Potter Group, Ely	OP
08216	D3286	11.80	Sheerness Steel, Sheerness	SS
08220	D3290	03.86	Steamtown Railway Centre	OP
08238	D3308	03.84	Dean Forest Railway	OP
08266	D3336	03.85	Keighley & Worth Valley Railway	OP
08288	D3358	01.83	Mid-Hants Railway	OP
08292	D3362	05.84	Deanside Transit, Glasgow	SU
08296	D3366	10.88	ABB Transportation, Crewe	OP
08308	D3378	02.92	South Yorkshire Railway	SU
08320	D3390	12.82	English China Clays, Fowey.	OP
08331	D3401	03.88	RFS Locomotives (For Hire)	OP
08345	D3415	10.83	Deanside Transit, Glasgow	OP
08350	D3420	01.84	Cheddleton Railway Centre	OP
08359	D3429	01.84	Peak Rail PLC	OP
08375	D3460	11.91	Bodmin & Wenford Railway	SB
08377	D3462	06.83	Dean Forest Railway	OP
08398	D3513	07.85	English China Clays, Rocks Driers, Bugle	OP
08416	D3531	02.92	RFS Locomotives (For Spares)	SU
08423	D3538	11.88	Trafford Park Estates, Manchester	OP
08436	D3551	01.92	South Yorkshire Railway	SU
08443	D3558	07.87	Bo'ness & Kinneil Railway	OP
08444	D3559	11.86	Bodmin & Wenford Railway	OP
08470	D3585	03.86	ABB Transportation, Crewe	OP
08471	D3586	09.85	Severn Valley Railway	OP
08476	D3591	09.85	Swanage Railway	OP
08479	D3594	11.91	East Lancashire Railway	OP
08490	D3605	12.85	Strathspey Railway	OP
08502	D3657	09.88	ICI, Wilton	OP
08503	D3658	09.88	ICI, Wilton	OP
08537	D3701	05.90	Flixborough Wharf, Flixborough	OP
08596	D3763	03.77	RFS Locomotives (For Hire)	OP
08598	D3765	11.86	PD Fuels, Gwaun-cae-Gurwen	OP
08602	D3769	03.86	ABB Transportation, Derby C & W	OP
08650	D3817	08.89	Foster Yeoman, Isle of Grain	OP
08652	D3819	06.92	Foster Yeoman, Merehead	OP
08669	D3836	05.89	Trafford Park Estates, Manchester	OP
08678	D3845	09.88	Glaxochem, Ulverston	OP
08704	D3871	11.90	Nene Valley Railway	OP
08728	D3896	09.87	Deanside Transit, Glasgow	OP
08736	D3904	09.87	Deanside Transit, Glasgow	OP
08743	D3911	03.93	RFS Locomotives (For Hire)	OP

08764	D3932	05.88	RFS Locomotives (For Hire)	OP
08769	D3937	04.89	Fire Services Training Centre, Moreton-in-Marsh	SU
08774	D3942	09.88	A.V. Dawson, Middlesborough	OP
08785	D3953	03.89	RFS Locomotives (For Hire)	OP
08816	D3984	02.86	Cobra, Middlesborough	OP
08846	D4014	10.89	ABB Transportation, Derby C & W	OP
08871	D4039	10.90	Humberside Sea & Land Services, Grimsby	OP
08874	D4042	02.92	RFS Locomotives (For Spares)	SU
08875	D4043	05.91	RFS Locomotives (For Spares)	SU
08876	D4044	09.91	RFS Locomotives (For Spares)	SU

CLASS 09   0-6-0 DE

Built: 1959 by BR at Darlington Works.
Engine: English Electric 6KT of 297 kW at 680 rpm.
Length over buffers: 8.915 m.   **Weight:** 47.10 t.
Extreme width: 2.915 m.   **Wheel Diameter:** 1372 mm.
Extreme height: 3.877 m.   **Maximum Permitted Speed:** 27.5 mph

| 09002 | D3666 | 09.92 | South Devon Railway | UR |

CLASS 10   0-6-0 DE

Built: 1957-62 by BR at Darlington Works.
Engine: Lister Blackstone ER6T of 261 kW at 750 rpm.
Length over buffers: 8.915 m.   **Weight:** 49.00 t.
Extreme width: 2.915 m.   **Wheel Diameter:** 1372 mm.
Extreme height: 3.877 m.   **Maximum Permitted Speed:** 20 mph.

	D3452	07.68	Bodmin & Wenford Railway	OP
	D3476	06.68	South Yorkshire Railway	SU
	D3489	04.68	Felixstowe Dock & Railway Company	OP
	D3639	07.69	Conakry, Guinea	EX
	D3649	07.69	Conakry, Guinea	EX
	D4067	12.70	Great Central Railway	OP
	D4092	09.68	South Yorkshire Railway	SU

CLASS 11   0-6-0 DE

Built: 1949-52 by BR at Derby Locomotive or Darlington Works.
Engine: English Electric 6KT of 260 kW at 680 rpm.
Length over buffers: 8.877 m.   **Weight:** 47.25 t.
Extreme width: **Wheel Diameter:** 1232 mm.
Extreme height: **Maximum Permitted Speed:** 20 mph.
Note: * Currently on loan to Cobra, Wakefield.

12049	10.71	Day & Son, Brentford	OP
12052	06.71	Scottish Industrial Railway Museum	SU
12061	10.71	Gwili Railway/Rheilffordd Gwili	OP
12071	10.71	South Yorkshire Railway	SU
12074	01.72	South Yorkshire Railway	SU
12077	10.71	Midland Railway Centre	OP
12082	10.71	South Yorkshire Railway*	OP
12083	10.71	Tilcon, Grassington	OP
12088	05.71	South Yorkshire Railway	SU
12093	05.71	Scottish Industrial Railway Centre	UR
12098	02.71	North Tyneside Steam Railway	UR
12099	07.71	Severn Valley Railway	UR
12131	07.71	North Norfolk Railway	OP

CLASS 12   0-6-0 DE

Built: 1949 by BR at Ashford Works.
Engine: English Electric 6KT of 260 kW at 680 rpm.
Length over buffers: 8.985 m.   **Weight:** 48.15 t.
Extreme width: **Wheel Diameter:** 1372 mm.
Extreme height: **Maximum Permitted Speed:** 27.5 mph

| 15224 | 10.71 | Lavender Line | OP |

CLASS 14   0-6-0 DH

Built: 1964-65 by BR at Swindon Works.
Engine: Paxman Ventura 6YJXL of 485 kW at 1500 rpm.
Length over buffers: 10.541 m.   **Weight:** 50.00 t.
Extreme width: **Wheel Diameter:** 1219 mm.
Extreme height: **Maximum Permitted Speed:** 40 mph.

D9500	04.69	South Yorkshire Railway	SU
D9502	04.69	South Yorkshire Railway	SU
D9504	04.68	Kent & East Sussex Steam Railway	OP
D9505	04.68	Maldegem, Belgium	EX
D9513	03.68	Embsay Steam Railway	OP
D9515	04.68	Charmartin, Madrid	SU
D9516	04.68	Nene Valley Railway	OP
D9518	04.69	Swanage Railway	SU
D9520	04.68	Rutland Railway Museum	OP
D9521	04.69	Swanage Railway	OP
D9521	04.68	Nene Valley Railway	OP
D9524	04.69	Bo'ness & Kinneil Railway	OP
D9525	04.68	Kent & East Sussex Steam Railway	OP

D9526	11.68	West Somerset Railway	OP
D9529	04.68	Nene Valley Railway	OP
D9531	12.67	East Lancashire Railway	OP
D9534	04.68	Milan, Italy	EX
D9537	04.68	Gloucestershire Warwickshire Railway	SU
D9539	04.68	Gloucestershire Warwickshire Railway	UR
D9548	04.68	Charmartin, Madrid	SU
D9549	04.68	Charmartin, Madrid	SU
D9551	04.68	West Somerset Railway	OP
D9553	04.68	Gloucestershire Warwickshire Railway	OP
D9555	04.68	Rutland Railway Museum	OP

CLASS 15   Bo-Bo DE

Built: 1960 by Clayton Equipment Company, Hatton.
Engine: Paxman 16YHXL of 597 kW.
Length over buffers: 12.887 m.   **Weight:** 68.00 t.
Extreme width: 2.794 m.   **Wheel Diameter:** 991 mm.
Extreme height: 3.810 m.   **Maximum Permitted Speed:** 60 mph.
Subsequent Number: ADB 968001 in Departmental Service.

| D8233 | 02.69 | Mangapps Farm Railway Museum | UR |

CLASS 17   Bo-Bo DE

Built: 1964 by Clayton Equipment Company, Hatton.
Engines: Two Paxman 6ZHXL of 336 kW each at 1500 rpm.
Length over buffers: 15.431 m.   **Weight:** 68.00 t.
Extreme width: 2.680 m.   **Wheel Diameter:** 1003 mm.
Extreme height: 3.861 m.   **Maximum Permitted Speed:** 60 mph.

| D8568 | 10.71 | Chinnor & Princes Risborough Railway | OP |

CLASS 20   Bo-Bo DE

Built: 1957-68 by English Electric, Vulcan Foundry, Newton-le-Willows or Robert Stephenson & Hawthorn, Darlington.
Engine: English Electric 8SVT Mk. II of 746 kW at 850 rpm.
Length over buffers: 14.259 m.   **Weight:** 72.05 (* 72.70, † 71.85) t.
Extreme width: 2.667 m.   **Wheel Diameter:** 1092 mm.
Extreme height: 3.851 m.   **Maximum Permitted Speed:** 75 mph.
Notes: 20172 has also carried 20305. 20194 has also carried 20307.

20001*	D8001	04.88	Midland Railway Centre	UR
20020*	D8020	10.90	Bo'ness & Kinneil Railway	OP
20031*	D8031	09.90	Keighley & Worth Valley Railway	OP

(Andrew Marshall)

▲ The unique BTH Class 15 D8233 at Mangapps Farm Railway Museum.

15

20035*	D8035	07.91	CFD, Autun, France	OP
20041*	D8041	11.88	Hunslet-Barclay Ltd. [20901]	ML
20047*	D8047	09.91	CTTG [04]	OP
20048*	D8048	11.90	Peak Rail PLC	OP
20050*	D8000	12.80	National Railway Museum	CE
20051†	D8051	02.91	RFS Locomotives (For Spares)	SU
20056†	D8056	10.90	Caledonian Railway	OP
20060†	D8060	11.88	Hunslet-Barclay Ltd. [20902]	ML
20063†	D8063	07.91	CFD, Autun, France	OP
20069†	D8069	05.91	County School	OP
20083†	D8083	01.89	Hunslet-Barclay Ltd. [20903]	ML
20084†	D8084	09.91	CTTG [31]	OP
20085†	D8085	03.91	RFS Locomotives (For Spares)	SU
20088†	D8088	09.91	CTTG [37]	OP
20095†	D8095	02.91	CTTG [29]	OP
20098†	D8098	06.91	Great Central Railway	OP
20101†	D8101	11.88	Hunslet-Barclay Ltd. [20904]	ML
20102†	D8102	09.91	CTTG [08]	OP
20105†	D8105	09.91	CTTG [36]	OP
20107†	D8107	01.91	East Lancashire Railway	OP
20108†	D8108	09.91	CTTG [01]	OP
20110†	D8110	09.91	South Devon Railway	OP
20113†	D8113	09.91	CTTG [32]	OP
20120†	D8120	09.91	CTTG [09]	OP
20127†	D8127	01.91	CTTG [38]	OP
20133	D8133	09.91	CTTG [05]	OP
20139	D8139	07.91	CFD, Autun, France	OP
20145	D8145	05.91	CTTG [39]	OP
20159	D8159	09.91	CTTG [10]	OP
20166	D8166	05.91	Bodmin & Wenford Railway	OP
20172	D8172	10.90	Bodmin & Wenford Railway	SB
20175	D8175	09.91	CTTG [07]	OP
20189	D8189	09.90	M.C. Metal Processing, Glasgow	OP
20194	D8194	09.91	CTTG [06]	OP
20197	D8197	11.91	Bodmin & Wenford Railway	SB
20205	D8305	12.89	East Lancashire Railway	SU
20206	D8306	04.91	County School	UR
20208	D8308	02.91	Midland Railway Centre	SU
20209	D8309	11.88	Hunslet-Barclay Ltd, Kilmarnock	SU
20219	D8319	01.89	Hunslet-Barclay Ltd. [20219]	ML
20220	D8320	11.87	Bodmin & Wenford Railway	SB
20225	D8325	01.89	Hunslet-Barclay Ltd. [20905]	ML
20227	D8327	10.90	Midland Railway Centre	OP
20228†	D8128	07.91	CFD, Autun, France	OP

CLASS 24 Bo-Bo DE

Built: 1959-60 by BR at Crewe Works.
Engine: Sulzer 6LDA28A of 866 kW at 750 rpm.
Length over buffers: 15.392 m.   **Weight:** 73.00 (* 78.70) t.
Extreme width: 2.769 m.   **Wheel Diameter:** 1143 mm.
Extreme height: 3.861 m.   **Maximum Permitted Speed:** 75 mph.
Subsequent Numbers: 24054 later became TDB 968008 in Departmental Service.
24061 later became TDB 968008 and then 97201 in Departmental Service.

24032*	D5032	07.76	North Yorkshire Moors Railway	OP
24054	D5054	07.76	East Lancashire Railway	OP
24061	D5061	08.75	North Tyneside Steam Railway	OP
24081	D5081	10.80	Southport Railway Centre	OP

CLASS 25 Bo-Bo DE

Built: 1963-67 by BR at Darlington or Derby Locomotive Works, or Beyer Peacock, Manchester.
Engine: Sulzer 6LDA28-B of 930 kW at 750 rpm.
Length over buffers: 15.392 m.   **Weight:** 71.45 (* 73.75) t.
Extreme width: 2.734 m.   **Wheel Diameter:** 1143 mm.
Extreme height: 3.861 m.   **Maximum Permitted Speed:** 90 mph.
Subsequent Numbers: 25901 (25262), 25904 (25283), 25909 (25309), 25912 (25322).

25035*	D5185	03.87	Northampton & Lamport Railway	UR
25057*	D5207	03.87	North Norfolk Railway	OP
25059*	D5209	03.87	Keighley & Worth Valley Railway	OP
25067*	D5217	12.82	Mid-Hants Railway	OP
25072*	D5222	12.85	Swindon & Cricklade Railway	OP
25083*	D5233	07.84	The Railway Age, Crewe	SU
25173	D7523	03.87	The Railway Age, Crewe	OP
25185	D7535	11.84	Paignton & Dartmouth Steam Railway	OP
25191	D7541	03.87	North Yorkshire Moors Railway	OP
25235*	D7585	03.85	Bo'ness & Kinneil Railway	OP
25244*	D7594	07.86	Nene Valley Railway	UR
25262	D7612	03.87	East Lancashire Railway	OP
25265	D7615	03.87	Peak Rail PLC	OP
25278	D7628	03.87	North Yorkshire Moors Railway	OP
25279	D7629	03.87	Llangollen Railway	OP
25283	D7633	03.87	Severn Valley Railway	OP
25309	D7659	09.86	East Lancashire Railway	OP
25313	D7663	03.87	Llangollen Railway	OP
25321	D7671	09.86	Midland Railway Centre	OP
25322	D7672	09.91	Cheddleton Railway Centre	OP

▲ Class 24 97201 "Experiment", whilst at Butterley in 1987.

(Andrew Marshall)

CLASS 27 Bo-Bo DE

Built: 1961-62 by Birmingham Railway Carriage & Wagon Company, Smethwick.
Engine: Sulzer 6LDA28-B of 930 kW at 750 rpm.
Length over buffers: 15.469 m.   **Weight:** 73.30 (* 71.20) t.
Extreme width: 2.692 m.   **Wheel Diameter:** 1092 mm.
Extreme height: 3.861 m.   **Maximum Permitted Speed:** 90 mph.
Subsequent Number: 27024 later became ADB 968028 in Departmental Service.
Notes: 27106 has also carried 27050. 27112 has also carried 27056. 27205 has
also carried 27123 and 27059. 27212 has also carried 27103 & 27066.

27001	D5347	07.87	Bo'ness & Kinneil Railway	OP
27005	D5351	07.87	Bo'ness & Kinneil Railway	OP
27007	D5353	01.85	Mid-Hants Railway	OP
27024*	D5370	07.87	Caledonian Railway	UR
27106	D5394	07.87	Strathspey Railway	UR
27112	D5401	02.87	Northampton & Lamport Railway	OP
27205	D5410	07.87	Birmingham Railway Museum	OP
27212	D5386	07.87	North Norfolk Railway	OP

CLASS 28 Co-Bo DE

Built: 1958 by Metropolitan Vickers, Stockton on Tees.
Engine: Crossley HSTV8 of 896 kW at 625 rpm.
Length over buffers: 17.259 m.   **Weight:** 97.00 t.
Extreme width: 2.807 m.   **Wheel Diameter:** 1003 mm.
Extreme height: 3.870 m.   **Maximum Permitted Speed:** 75 mph.
Subsequent Numbers: S15705, TDB 968006 in Departmental Service.

D5705	09.68	Peak Rail PLC	UR

CLASS 31 A1A-A1A DE

Built: 1957 by Brush Traction, Loughborough.
Engine: Mirlees JVS12T of 933 kW.
Length over buffers: 17.297 m.   **Weight:** 104.00 t.
Extreme width: 2.667 m.   **Powered Wheel Diameter:** 1092 mm.
Extreme height: 3.848 m.   **Unpowered Wheel Diameter:** 1003mm.
Maximum Permitted Speed: 75 mph.

31018	D5500	07.76	Steamtown Railway Centre	OP

CLASS 33 Bo-Bo DE

Built: 1960-62 by Birmingham Railway Carriage & Wagon Company, Smethwick.
Engine: Sulzer 8LDA28 of 1160 kW at 750 rpm.

Length over buffers: 15.240 m.   **Weight:** 76.45 (* 76.25) t.
Extreme width: 2.743 (* 2.642) m.   **Wheel Diameter:** 1092 mm.
Extreme height: 3.861 m.   **Maximum Permitted Speed:** 85 mph.

33034	D6552	02.88	Ministry of Defence, Ludgershall	UR
33056	D6574	02.91	Ministry of Defence, Ludgershall	UR
33111	D6528	06.91	St. Leonards Railway Engineering	UR
33203*	D6588	04.91	Ministry of Defence, Ludgershall	UR

33035   33021   33108   33102   33110

CLASS 35   B-B DH

Built: 1962-63 by Beyer Peacock, Manchester.
Engine: Maybach MD870 of 1300 kW at 1500 rpm.
Length over buffers: 15.761 m.   **Weight:** 74.00 t.
Extreme width: 2.654 m.   **Wheel Diameter:** 1143 mm.
Extreme height: 3.926 m.   **Maximum Permitted Speed:** 90 mph.

D7017	03.75	West Somerset Railway	OP
D7018	03.75	West Somerset Railway	OP
D7029	02.75	North Yorkshire Moors Railway	SU
D7076	05.73	East Lancashire Railway	UR

CLASS 40   1Co-Co1 DE

Built: 1958-61 by English Electric, Vulcan Foundry, Newton-le-Willows or Robert Stephenson & Hawthorn, Darlington.
Engine: English Electric 16SVT Mk. II of 1493 kW at 850 rpm.
Length over buffers: 21.184 m.   **Weight:** 133.00 t.
Extreme width: 2.743 m.   **Powered Wheel Diameter:** 1143 mm.
Extreme height: 3.921 m.   **Unpowered Wheel Diameter:** 914 mm.
Maximum Permitted Speed: 90 mph.
Subsequent Numbers: 97407 (40012), 97408 (40118), 97406 (40135) in Departmental Service.

40012	D212	02.85	Midland Railway Centre	OP
40013	D213	01.85	South Yorkshire Railway	UR
40106	D306	04.83	Nene Valley Railway	OP
40118	D318	02.85	Birmingham Railway Museum	UR
40122	D200	04.88	National Railway Museum	OP
40135	D335	01.85	East Lancashire Railway	OP
40145	D345	06.83	East Lancashire Railway	UR

CLASS 42   B-B DH

Built: 1960-61 by BR at Swindon Works.
Engines: Two Maybach MD650 of 820 kW each at 1530 rpm

▲ NRM owned Class 31 D5518 is on loan to Steamtown Railway Centre. (Robert Greengrass)

21

Length over buffers: 18.288 m.   **Weight:** 78.00 t.
Extreme width: 2.654 m.   **Wheel Diameter:** 1003 mm.
Extreme height: 3.899 m.   **Maximum Permitted Speed:** 90 mph.

D821	12.72	Severn Valley Railway		OP
D832	12.72	East Lancashire Railway		OP

CLASS 43   Bo-Bo DE

Built: 1972 by British Rail Engineering Ltd., Crewe Works.
Engine: Paxman Valenta 12RP200L of 1680 kW at 1500 rpm.
Length over buffers: 17.145 m.   **Weight:** 66.00 t.
Extreme width: 2.743 m.   **Wheel Diameter:** 1016 mm.
Extreme height: 3.912 m.   **Maximum Permitted Speed:** 125 mph.
Original Number: 41001.
Subsequent Number: ADB 975812 in Departmental Service.

43000	11.76	National Railway Museum	IE

CLASS 44   1Co-Co1 DE

Built: 1959 by BR at Derby Locomotive Works.
Engine: Sulzer 12LDA28A of 1716 kW at 750 rpm.
Length over buffers: 20.701 m.   **Weight:** 133.00 t.
Extreme width: 2.783 m.   **Powered Wheel Diameter:** 1143 mm.
Extreme height: 3.915 m.   **Unpowered Wheel Diameter:** 914 mm.
Maximum Permitted Speed: 90 mph.

44004	D4	11.80	Midland Railway Centre	OP
44008	D8	11.80	Peak Rail PLC	UR

CLASS 45   1Co-Co1 DE

Built: 1960-62 by BR at Derby Locomotive or Crewe Works.
Engine: Sulzer 12LDA28B of 1866 kW at 750 rpm.
Length over buffers: 20.701 m.   **Weight:** 136.10 t.
Extreme width: 2.783 m.   **Powered Wheel Diameter:** 1143 mm.
Extreme height: 3.915 m.   **Unpowered Wheel Diameter:** 914 mm.
Maximum Permitted Speed: 90 mph.

45060	D100	12.85	Peak Rail PLC	OP
45105	D86	05.87	Peak Rail PLC	UR
45108	D120	08.87	The Railway Age, Crewe	OP
45112	D61	05.87	East Lancashire Railway	UR
45118	D67	05.87	Northampton & Lamport Railway	UR
45121	D18	11.87	ABB Transportation, Derby C & W	SU
45125	D123	05.87	Dairycoates Depot, Hull	UR

45132	D22	05.87	Mid-Hants Railway	UR
45133	D40	05.87	Midland Railway Centre	OP
45135	D99	03.87	Peak Rail PLC	OP
45149	D135	09.87	Lancastrian Carriage & Wagon Co., Heysham	UR

CLASS 46   1Co-Co1 DE

Built: 1961-63 by BR at Derby Locomotive Works.
Engine: Sulzer 12LDA28B of 1866 kW at 750 rpm.
Length over buffers: 20.701 m.   **Weight:** 138.00 t.
Extreme width: 2.783 m.   **Powered Wheel Diameter:** 1143 mm.
Extreme height: 3.915 m.   **Unpowered Wheel Diameter:** 914 mm.
Maximum Permitted Speed: 90 mph.
Subsequent Numbers: 97403 (46035), 97404 (46045) in Departmental Service.

46010	D147	11.84	Llangollen Railway	SU
46035	D172	11.84	The Railway Age, Crewe	UR
46045	D182	11.84	Midland Railway Centre	UR

CLASS 47   Co-Co DE

Built: 1962-65 by Brush Traction, Loughborough or BR, Crewe Works.
Engine: Sulzer 12LDA28C of 2052 kW at 800 rpm.
Length over buffers: 19.355 m.   **Weight:** 116.90 (* 115.35) t.
Extreme width: 2.794 m.   **Wheel Diameter:** 1143 mm.
Extreme height: 3.896 m.   **Maximum Permitted Speed:** 95 mph.

47192*	D1842	05.88	The Railway Age, Crewe	OP
47401	D1500	06.92	Midland Railway Centre	OP
47402	D1501	06.92	East Lancashire Railway	OP
47403	D1502	09.86	The Railway Age, Crewe	UR
47449*	D1566	05.93		SB

CLASS 50   Co-Co DE

Built: 1967-68 by English Electric, Vulcan Foundry, Newton-le-Willows.
Engine: English Electric 16SVT of 2015 kW at 850 rpm.
Length over buffers: 20.879 m.   **Weight:** 115.05 t.
Extreme width: 2.775 m.   **Wheel Diameter:** 1092 mm.
Extreme height: 3.956 m.   **Maximum Permitted Speed:** 100 mph.
Subsequent Numbers: 50149 (50049).

50002	D402	09.91	Paignton & Dartmouth Steam Railway	OP
50008	D408	06.92	BR, Longsight Diesel Depot	UR
50015	D415	06.92	East Lancashire Railway	OP
50017	D417	09.91	The Railway Age, Crewe	UR

50019	D419	09.90	Spa Railway	UR
50021	D421	04.90	Gloucestershire Warwickshire Railway	UR
50026	D426	12.90	Mid-Hants Railway	UR
50027	D427	07.91	Mid-Hants Railway	OP
50031	D431	08.91	St. Leonards Railway Engineering	OP
50035	D435	08.90	St. Leonards Railway Engineering	UR
50042	D442	10.90	Bodmin & Wenford Railway	OP
50043	D443	02.91	Birmingham Railway Museum	CE
50044	D444	01.91	St. Leonards Railway Engineering	UR
50049	D449	08.91	Allied Steel & Wire, Cardiff	UR

CLASS 52   C-C DH

Built: 1962-63 by BR at Swindon or Crewe Works.
Engines: Two Maybach MD655 of 1007 kW each at 1500 rpm.
Length over buffers: 20.726 m.   **Weight:** 108.00 t.
Extreme width: 2.743 m.   **Wheel Diameter:** 1092 mm.
Extreme height: 3.959 m.   **Maximum Permitted Speed:** 90 mph.
Note: D1010 is preserved as D1035 "Western Yeoman"

	D1010	02.77	West Somerset Railway	UR
	D1013	02.77	Severn Valley Railway	OP
	D1015	12.76	BR Old Oak Common Depot	UR
	D1023	02.77	National Railway Museum	CE
	D1041	02.77	East Lancashire Railway	OP
	D1048	02.77	Bodmin & Wenford Railway	UR
	D1062	08.74	Severn Valley Railway	OP

CLASS 55   Co-Co DE

Built: 1961 by English Electric, Vulcan Foundry, Newton-le-Willows.
Engines: Two Napier Deltic D18-25 of 1230 kW each at 1500 rpm.
Length over buffers: 21.184 m.   **Weight:** 99.90 t.
Extreme width: 2.680 m.   **Wheel Diameter:** 1092 mm.
Extreme height: 3.937 m.   **Maximum Permitted Speed:** 100 mph.

55002	D9002	01.82	National Railway Museum	OP
55009	D9009	01.82	ICI, Wilton	UR
55015	D9015	01.82	Midland Railway Centre	OP
55016	D9016	12.81	BR Old Oak Common Depot	OP
55019	D9019	12.81	Great Central Railway	OP
55022	D9000	01.82	BR Old Oak Common Depot	OP

▲ Maroon liveried Class 52 D1062 works a service on the Severn Valley Railway in 1988. (Andrew Marshall)

CLASS 71   Bo-Bo OE/RE

Built: 1959 by BR at Doncaster Works.
Supply System: 660-750 V dc third rail or overhead.
Traction Motors: Electric. Four English Electric type 532.
Continuous Rating: 1716 kW at 69.6 mph.
Length over buffers: 15.418 m.   **Weight:** 77.00 t.
Extreme width: 2.821 m.   **Wheel Diameter:** 1219 mm.
Extreme height: 3.988 m.   **Maximum Permitted Speed:** 90 mph.
71001   E5001   11.77   National Railway Museum   ML

CLASS 73   Bo-Bo ED

Built: 1962 by BR at Eastleigh Works.
Engine: English Electric 4SRKT of 448 kW at 850 rpm.
Supply System: 660-750 V dc third rail.
Continuous Rating: 1060 kW at 55.5 mph on electric power.
Length over buffers: 16.358 m.   **Weight:** 75.10 t.
Extreme width: 2.642 m.   **Wheel Diameter:** 1016 mm.
Extreme height: 3.796 m.   **Maximum Permitted Speed:** 80 mph.
Note: On extended loan from British Rail.
73003   E6003   Mid-Hants Railway   ML

CLASS 76   Bo+Bo OE

Built: 1951 by BR at Gorton Works.
Supply System: 1500 v dc overhead.
Traction Motors: Four Metropolitan Vickers type 486.
Continuous Rating: 970 kW at 56 mph.
Length over buffers: 15.392 m.   **Weight:** 87.30 t.
Extreme width: 2.743 m.   **Wheel Diameter:** 1270 mm.
Extreme height: 4.191 m.   **Maximum Permitted Speed:** 65 mph.
Original Number: 26020.
76020   E26020   07.81   National Railway Museum   IE

CLASS 77   Co-Co OE

Built: 1953-54 by BR at Gorton Works.
Supply System: 1500 V dc overhead.
Traction Motors: Six Metropolitan Vickers type 146.
Continuous Rating: 78 kN at 23 mph.
Length over buffers: 17.983 m.   **Weight:** 102.50 t.
Extreme width: **Wheel Diameter:** 1092 mm.

(Robert Greengrass)

▲ Class 55 Deltic D9000 on display at an Open Day at Coalville in 1989.

Extreme height: **Maximum Permitted Speed:** 90 mph.
Original Numbers: 27000/01/03 respectively.
Subsequent Numbers: NS 1502/05/01 respectively.

E27000	09.68	BR Ilford Depot		SS
E27001	09.68	Museum of Science & Industry, Manchester		CE
E27003	09.68	Rotterdam, The Netherlands.		OP

CLASS 81 Bo-Bo OE

Built: 1960 by Birmingham Railway Carriage & Wagon Company, Smethwick.
Supply System: 25 kV ac 50 Hz overhead.
Traction Motors: Four AEI type 189.
Continuous Rating: 2388 kW at 71 mph.
Length over buffers: 17.221 m. **Weight:** 80.00 t.
Extreme width: 2.648 m. **Wheel Diameter:** 1219 mm.
Extreme height: 3.977 m. **Maximum Permitted Speed:** 100 mph.

81002	E3003	10.90	The Railway Age, Crewe	UR

CLASS 82 Bo-Bo OE

Built: 1961 by Beyer Peacock, Manchester.
Supply System: 25 kV ac 50 Hz overhead.
Traction Motors: Four AEI type 189.
Continuous Rating: 2463 kW at 73 mph.
Length over buffers: 17.069 m. **Weight:** 77.45 t.
Extreme width: 2.667 m. **Wheel Diameter:** 1219 mm.
Extreme height: 3.977 m. **Maximum Permitted Speed:** 100 mph.

82008	E3054	12.87	The Railway Age, Crewe	IE

CLASS 83 Bo-Bo OE

Built: 1961 by English Electric, Vulcan Foundry, Newton-le-Willows.
Supply System: 25 kV ac 50 Hz overhead.
Traction Motors: Four English Electric type 535A.
Length over buffers: 16.002 m. **Weight:** 74.50 t.
Extreme width: 2.661 m. **Wheel Diameter:** 1219 mm.
Extreme height: 3.978 m. **Maximum Permitted Speed:** 100 mph.

83012	E3035	03.89	Lancastrian Carriage & Wagon Co., Heysham	UR

CLASS 84 Bo-Bo OE

Built: 1960 by North British Locomotive Company, Glasgow.
Supply System: 25 kV ac 50 Hz overhead.

Traction Motors: Four GEC type WT501.
Continuous Rating: 2313 kW at 66 mph.

Length over buffers: 16.320 m.	**Weight:** 77.00 t.
Extreme width: 2.648 m.	**Wheel Diameter:** 1219 mm.
Extreme height: 3.978 m.	**Maximum Permitted Speed:** 100 mph.

Note: On extended loan from British Rail.

84001　E3036　01.79　National Railway Museum　　　IE

CLASS 85　　　　　　　　　　Bo-Bo OE

Built: 1961 by BR at Doncaster Works.
Supply System: 25 kV ac 50 Hz overhead.
Traction Motors: Four AEI type 189.
Continuous Rating: 2388 kW at 71 mph.

Length over buffers: 17.221 m.	**Weight:** 79.65 t.
Extreme width: 2.648 m.	**Wheel Diameter:** 1219 mm.
Extreme height: 3.978 m.	**Maximum Permitted Speed:** 100 mph.

Subsequent Number: 85101.

85006　E3061　11.92　The Railway Age, Crewe　　　SU

CLASS 89　　　　　　　　　　Co-Co OE

Built: 1986 by BREL, Crewe.
Supply System: 25 kV ac 50 Hz overhead.
Traction Motors: Six Brush type TM2201A.
Continuous Rating: 3200 kW at 91.8 mph.

Length over buffers: 19.798 m.	**Weight:** 102.25 t.
Extreme width: 2.736 m.	**Wheel Diameter:** 1070 mm.
Extreme height: 3.977 m.	**Maximum Permitted Speed:** 125 mph.

89001　　　07.92　Midland Railway Centre　　　UR

CLASS 97/6　　　　　　　　　0-6-0 DE

Built: 1952 by Ruston & Hornsby, Lincoln.
Engine: Ruston 6VPH of 123 kW.

Length over buffers: 7.620 m.	**Weight:** 30.20 t.
Extreme width: 2.565 m.	**Wheel Diameter:** 978 mm.
Extreme height: 3.353 m.	**Maximum Permitted Speed:** 20 mph.

97650　PWM650　04.87　Lincoln Enterprise Agency, Lincoln　　　IE

▲ Unique Class 89001 whilst in service on the East Coast route.

(Andrew Marshall)

CLASS 98/1 0-6-0 DH

Built: 1987 by Brecon Mountain Railway, Pant.
Gauge: 597 mm.
Engine: Caterpillar 3304T of 105 kW.

Length over buffers: 5.029 m.	**Weight:** 12.75 t.
Extreme width:	**Wheel Diameter:** 610 mm.
Extreme height:	**Maximum Permitted Speed:** 15 mph.

10	04.89	Vale of Rheidol Railway	OP

1.2 LOCOMOTIVES NOT CLASSIFIED UNDER THE TOPS SYSTEM

UNCLASSIFIED A1A-A1A GTE

Built: 1949 by Brown Boveri, Switzerland.
Turbine: Brown Boveri of 1866 kW.

Length over buffers: 19.215 m.	**Weight:** 119.15 t.
Extreme width: 2.807 m.	**Powered Wheel Diameter:** 1232 mm.
Extreme height: 4.064 m.	**Unpowered Wheel Diameter:** 965 mm.
Maximum Permitted Speed: 90 mph.	

18000	02.60	UIC ORE Testing Station, Vienna, Austria	IE

UNCLASSIFIED 0-6-0 DM

Built: 1961 by Hudswell Clarke, Leeds.
Engine: Gardner 8L3 of 152 kW at 1200 rpm.

Length over buffers: 8.007 m.	**Weight:** 34.20 t.
Extreme width:	**Wheel Diameter:** 1067 mm.
Extreme height:	**Maximum Permitted Speed:** 24 mph.

D2511	12.67	Keighley & Worth Valley Railway	OP

UNCLASSIFIED 0-4-0 DH

Built: 1960 by North British Locomotive Company, Glasgow.
Engine: MAN W6V 17.5/22A of 168 kW at 1100 rpm.

Length over buffers: 7.455 m.	**Weight:** 36.00 t.
Extreme width:	**Wheel Diameter:** 1143 mm.

▲ Narrow gauge Class 98/1 No. 10 at Aberystwyth.

(Andrew Marshall)

			Maximum Permitted Speed: 15 mph.
Extreme height:			
D2767	06.67	East Lancashire Railway	OP
D2774	06.67	East Lancashire Railway	UR

UNCLASSIFIED   Bo-Bo OE/RE

Built: 1903 by North Eastern Railway, Gateshead Works.
Supply System: 600-630 V dc third rail or overhead.
Traction Motors: Four BTH design.

Length over buffers: 11.506 m.	**Weight:** 46.00 t.
Extreme width:	**Wheel Diameter:** 914 mm.
Extreme height:	**Maximum Permitted Speed:**

Original Number: Originally NER 1, then LNER 6480 and BR 26500.

E26500	02.64	National Railway Museum	CE

UNCLASSIFIED   Bo RE

Built: 1898 by Siemens, London.
Supply System: 500 v dc inner live rail.
Traction Motors: Two Siemens of 45 kW.

Length over buffers:	**Weight:** 22.00 t.
Extreme width:	**Wheel Diameter:** 1016 mm.
Extreme height:	**Maximum Permitted Speed:**

Original Number: Originally un-numbered, then Southern Railway 75s.

DS75	05.68	National Railway Museum	CE

UNCLASSIFIED   Bo BE

Built: 1917 by North Staffordshire Railway, Stoke-on-Trent Works.
Supply System: 108 cell battery.
Traction Motors: Two BTH of 31 kW each.

Length over buffers:	**Weight:** 17.00 t.
Extreme width:	**Wheel Diameter:** 940 mm.
Extreme height:	**Maximum Permitted Speed:**

Original Number: Originally numbered NSR 1.

BEL 2	03.63	National Railway Museum	CE

UNCLASSIFIED   0-4-0 DM

Built: 1958 by Ruston & Hornsby, Lincoln.
Gauge: 914 mm. (For Beeston Sleeper Depot).
Engine: Ruston 4YCL of 36 kW at 1375 rpm.

Length over buffers: 4.140 m.   Weight: 8.20 t.
Extreme width: Wheel Diameter: 762 mm.
Extreme height: Maximum Permitted Speed:

| ED10 | 02.65 | Irchester Narrow Gauge Railway Museum | | UR |

UNCLASSIFIED   0-4-0 DM

Built: 1957 by Ruston & Hornsby, Lincoln.
Gauge: 457 mm. (For BR, Horwich Works).
Engine: Ruston 2VSH of 15 kW at 1200 rpm.
Length over buffers: Weight: 3.50 t.
Extreme width: Wheel Diameter: 414 mm.
Extreme height: Maximum Permitted Speed:

| ZM32 | 03.64 | Narrow Gauge Railway Centre | |

UNCLASSIFIED   0-4-0 DM

Built: 1956-57 by Ruston & Hornsby, Lincoln.
Gauge: 610 mm. (For Chesterton Junction Central Materials Depot).
Engine: Ruston 3VSHL of 24 kW.
Length over buffers: 2.261 m.   Weight: 4.00 t.
Extreme width: Wheel Diameter: 414 mm.
Extreme height: Maximum Permitted Speed:

| 85049 | ??.86 | Vobster Light Railway | | OP |
| 85051 | ??.86 | Cadeby Light Railway | | |

1.3 LOCOMOTIVES WITHDRAWN PRIOR TO 1st JANUARY 1948

UNCLASSIFIED   0-4-0 DM

Built: 1919 by Motor Rail & Tram Car Company, Bedford, for the Lancashire & Yorkshire Railway.
Engine: Dorman 4JO of 30 kW (Petrol).
Length over buffers: 4.064 m.   Weight: 8.00 t.
Extreme width: Wheel Diameter: 940 mm.
Extreme height: Maximum Permitted Speed: 7 mph.

| 1 | 11.30 | Chasewater Light Railway | |

UNCLASSIFIED   0-4-0 DM

Built: 1934 by English Electric, Preston, for the London Midland & Scottish Railway.
Engine: Allan 8RS18 of 119 kW at 1200 rpm.

Length over buffers: 7.277 m.	**Weight:** 25.40 t.
Extreme width:	**Wheel Diameter:** 914 mm.
Extreme height:	**Maximum Permitted Speed:** 12 mph.

Subsequent Number: War Department 240.

7050	03.43	Museum of Army Transport	CE

UNCLASSIFIED   0-6-0 DM

Built: 1932 by Hunslet Engine Company, Leeds, for the London Midland & Scottish Railway.
Engine: MAN 6 cylinder of 112 kW at 900 rpm.

Length over buffers: 7.061 m.	**Weight:** 21.40 t.
Extreme width:	**Wheel Diameter:** 914 mm.
Extreme height:	**Maximum Permitted Speed:** 30 mph.

Subsequent Number: 7401.

7051	12.45	Middleton Railway	OP

UNCLASSIFIED   0-6-0 DE

Built: 1935 by Hawthorn Leslie, Newcastle-upon-Tyne, for the London Midland & Scottish Railway.
Engine: English Electric 6KT of 261 kW at 675 rpm.

Length over buffers: 8.706 m.	**Weight:** 51.45 t.
Extreme width:	**Wheel Diameter:** 1232 mm.
Extreme height:	**Maximum Permitted Speed:** 30 mph.

Subsequent Number: War Department 18.

7069	12.40	Blue Circle, Hamworthy	UR

UNCLASSIFIED   0-6-0 DE

Built: 1941 by London Midland & Scottish Railway, Derby Locomotive Works.
Engine: English Electric 6KT of 261 kW at 680 rpm.

Length over buffers: 9.893 m.	**Weight:** 53.50 t.
Extreme width:	**Wheel Diameter:** 1295 mm.
Extreme height:	**Maximum Permitted Speed:** 20 mph.

Subsequent Numbers: WD 52, FS 700.001 (7103); WD 55, FS 700.003 (7106).

7103	12.42	FSAS, Arezzo, Italy	OP
7106	12.42	Car"boni, Colico, Italy	OP

(Robert Greengrass)

▲ Hunslet 0-6-0 LMS 7401 at work on the Middleton Railway.

1.4 FORMER WAR DEPARTMENT LOCOMOTIVES

Note: Dates shown in this section are dates withdrawn from War Department/Ministry of Defence service.

UNCLASSIFIED   0-6-0 DE

Built: 1945 by London Midland & Scottish Railway, Derby Locomotive Works.
Engine: English Electric 6KT of 261 kW at 680 rpm.

Length over buffers: 8.877 m.	**Weight:** 47.25 t.	
Extreme width:	**Wheel Diameter:** 1232 mm.	
Extreme height:	**Maximum Permitted Speed:** 20 mph.	

Subsequent Numbers: NS 508 (70269).

70269	03.46	Utrecht Railway Museum, The Netherlands	CE
70272	??.80	Lakeside & Haverthwaite Railway	OP

1.5 MANUFACTURERS PROTOTYPE LOCOMOTIVES NOT TAKEN INTO BR STOCK

UNCLASSIFIED   Co-Co DE

Built: 1954 by English Electric, Preston.
Engines: Two Napier Deltic D18-25 of 1230 kW each at 1500 rpm.

Length over buffers: 20.117 m.	**Weight:** 106.00 t.
Extreme width: 2.680 m.	**Wheel Diameter:** 1092 mm.
Extreme height: 3.924 m.	**Maximum Permitted Speed:** 90 mph.

DELTIC	03.61	Science Museum, London	IE

UNCLASSIFIED   0-6-0 DE

Built: 1956 by English Electric, Vulcan Foundry.
Engine: English Electric 6RKT of 373 kW at 750 rpm.

Length over buffers:	**Weight:** 48.00 t.
Extreme width:	**Wheel Diameter:** 1219 mm.

Extreme height:
Original Number: D226.

D0226	10.60	Keighley & Worth Valley Railway	OP

UNCLASSIFIED 0-4-0 DH

Built: 1954 by North British Locomotive Company, Glasgow.
Engine: Paxman 6VRPHXL of 233 kW at 1250 rpm.
Length over buffers: **Weight:**
Extreme width: **Wheel Diameter:** 1016 mm.
Extreme height: **Maximum Permitted Speed:** 12 mph.

TOM	??.55	Telford Horsehay Steam Trust
TIGER	??.55	Bo'ness & Kinneil Railway

PART TWO - DIESEL MULTIPLE UNITS

2.1 "FIRST GENERATION" VEHICLES

CLASS 103 DMBS

Built: 1958 by Park Royal Vehicles, London.
Engines: Two horizontal AEC 220 type of 112 kW at 1800 rpm.
Transmission: Mechanical.
Length over buffers: 18.491 m.   **Weight:** 33.45 t.
Extreme width: 2.724 m.   **Seats:** 52.
Extreme height: 3.766 m.   **Toilet:** Not equipped.
Maximum Permitted Speed: 70 mph.

50397	02.71	Battlefield Steam Railway	SU
50413	12.72	West Somerset Railway	SU

UNCLASSIFIED DMBS

Built: 1957-58 by D. Wickham, Ware.
Engines: Two horizontal Leyland 680/1 type of 112 kW at 1800 rpm.
Transmission: Mechanical.
Length over buffers: 18.339 m.   **Weight:** 27.00 t.
Extreme width: 2.819 m.   **Seats:** 59.
Extreme height: 3.835 m.   **Toilet:** Not equipped.
Maximum Permitted Speed: 70 mph.

50415	09.61	Trinidad Government Railways	EX
50416	10.67	Llangollen Railway	UR
50419	09.61	Trinidad Government Railways	EX

CLASS 126 DMSL

Built: 1959 by BR at Swindon Works.
Engines: Two horizontal AEC 220 type of 112 kW at 1800 rpm.
Transmission: Mechanical.
Length over buffers: 20.155 m.   **Weight:** 38.85 t.
Extreme width: 2.819 m.   **Seats:** 64.
Extreme height: 3.886 m.   **Toilet:** 1.
Maximum Permitted Speed: 70 mph.

| 51017 | 12.82 | Caledonian Railway | SU |

CLASS 126 DMBSL

Built: 1959 by BR at Swindon Works.
Engines: Two horizontal AEC 220 type of 112 kW at 1800 rpm.
Transmission: Mechanical.
Length over buffers: 20.155 m.   **Weight:** 37.35 t.
Extreme width: 2.819 m.   **Seats:** 52.
Extreme height: 3.886 m.   **Toilets:** 2.
Maximum Permitted Speed: 70 mph.

| 51043 | 12.82 | Caledonian Railway | SU |

CLASS 100 DMBS

Built: 1957 by Gloucester Railway Carriage & Wagon Company, Gloucester
Engines: Two horizontal AEC 220 type of 112 kW at 1800 rpm.
Transmission: Mechanical.
Length over buffers: 18.491 m.   **Weight:** 30.00 t.
Extreme width: 2.743 m.   **Seats:** 52.
Extreme height: 3.861 m.   **Toilet:** Not equipped.
Maximum Permitted Speed: 70 mph.

| 51118 | 10.72 | West Somerset Railway | SS |

CLASS 116 DMBS

Built: 1958 by BR at Derby C & W Works.
Engines: Two horizontal Leyland type 680/1 of 112 kW at 1800 rpm.
Transmission: Mechanical.
Length over buffers: 20.447 m.   **Weight:** 35.95 t.

Extreme width: 2.819 m.   **Seats:** 65.
Extreme height: 3.861 m.   **Toilet:** Not equipped.
Maximum Permitted Speed: 70 mph.

51135	05.92	PD Fuels, Coed Bach Disposal Point	SU

CLASS 116   DMS

Built: 1958 by BR at Derby C & W Works.
Engines: Two horizontal Leyland type 680/1 of 112 kW at 1800 rpm.
Transmission: Mechanical.
Length over buffers: 20.447 m.   **Weight:** 35.95 t.
Extreme width: 2.819 m.   **Seats:** 95.
Extreme height: 3.861 m.   **Toilet:** Not equipped.
Maximum Permitted Speed: 70 mph.

51148	06.92	PD Fuels, Coed Bach Disposal Point	SU

CLASS 101   DMBS

Built: 1959 by Metropolitan Cammell, Birmingham.
Engines: Two horizontal AEC 220 type of 112 kW at 1800 rpm.
Transmission: Mechanical.
Length over buffers: 18.491 m.   **Weight:** 32.05 t.
Extreme width: 2.819 m.   **Seats:** 52.
Extreme height: 3.848 m.   **Toilet:** Not equipped.
Maximum Permitted Speed: 70 mph.

51203	09.89	Darlington Railway Centre & Museum	SU

CLASS 105   DMBS

Built: 1959 by Cravens, Sheffield.
Engines: Two horizontal AEC 220 type of 112 kW at 1800 rpm.
Transmission: Mechanical.
Length over buffers: 18.644 m.   **Weight:** 30.00 t.
Extreme width: 2.819 m.   **Seats:** 52.
Extreme height: 3.772 m.   **Toilet:** Not equipped.
Maximum Permitted Speed: 70 mph.

51485	05.81	West Somerset Railway	OP

CLASS 108   DMCL

Built: 1959-60 by BR at Derby C & W Works.
Engines: Two horizontal Leyland 680/1 or 680/13 type of 112 kW at 1800 rpm.

Transmission: Mechanical.
Length over buffers: 18.491 m.   **Weight:** 28.50 t.
Extreme width: 2.819 m.   **Seats:** 12 1st, 52 2nd.
Extreme height: 3.874 m.   **Toilet:** 1.
Maximum Permitted Speed: 70 mph.

51562	06.92	National Railway Museum	UR
51565	03.92	Keighley & Worth Valley Railway	OP
51566	12.92	Peak Rail PLC	UR
51568	02.93		SB
51571	09.92	Kent & East Sussex Steam Railway	
51572	01.93	East Kent Light Railway	

CLASS 127   DMBS

Built: 1959 by BR at Derby C & W Works.
Engines: Two Rolls Royce C8NFLH823 type of 178 kW at 1800 rpm.
Transmission: Hydraulic.
Length over buffers: 20.447 m.   **Weight:** 39.85 t.
Extreme width: 2.819 m.   **Seats:** 76.
Extreme height: 3.874 m.   **Toilet:** Not equipped.
Maximum Permitted Speed: 70 mph.

51592	01.84	Paignton & Dartmouth Steam Railway	OP
51604	08.83	Paignton & Dartmouth Steam Railway	OP
51616	01.84	Great Central Railway	OP
51618	12.83	Llangollen Railway	OP
51622	01.84	Great Central Railway	OP

CLASS 115   DMBS

Built: 1960 by BR at Derby C & W Works.
Engines: Two horizontal Leyland Albion 902 type of 172 kW at 1800 rpm.
Transmission: Mechanical.
Length over buffers: 20.447 m.   **Weight:** 37.85 t.
Extreme width: 2.819 m.   **Seats:** 78.
Extreme height: 3.874 m.   **Toilet:** Not equipped.
Maximum Permitted Speed: 70 mph.

51655	08.92	Lavender Line	UR
51663	08.92	West Somerset Railway	
51669	03.92	County School	UR
51677	08.92	Lavender Line	UR

CLASS 110 — DMBC

Built: 1961 by Birmingham Railway Carriage & Wagon Company, Smethwick.
Engines: Two Rolls Royce C6NFLH138D type of 134 kW at 1800 rpm.
Transmission: Mechanical.
Length over buffers: 18.485 m.   **Weight:** 32.00 t.
Extreme width: 2.819 m.   **Seats:** 12 1st, 33 2nd.
Extreme height: 3.835 m.   **Toilet:** Not equipped.
Maximum Permitted Speed: 70 mph.

| 51813 | 03.90 | East Lancashire Railway | OP |

CLASS 110 — DMCL

Built: 1961 by Birmingham Railway Carriage & Wagon Company, Smethwick.
Engines: Two Rolls Royce C6NFLH138D type of 134 kW at 1800 rpm.
Transmission: Mechanical.
Length over buffers: 18.485 m.   **Weight:** 32.00 t.
Extreme width: 2.819 m.   **Seats:** 12 1st, 54 2nd.
Extreme height: 3.835 m.   **Toilet:** 1.
Maximum Permitted Speed: 70 mph.

| 51842 | 02.90 | East Lancashire Railway | OP |

CLASS 115 — DMBS

Built: 1960 by BR at Derby C & W Works.
Engines: Two horizontal Leyland Albion 902 type of 172 kW at 1800 rpm.
Transmission: Mechanical.
Length over buffers: 20.447 m.   **Weight:** 37.85 t.
Extreme width: 2.819 m.   **Seats:** 78.
Extreme height: 3.874 m.   **Toilet:** Not equipped.
Maximum Permitted Speed: 70 mph.

| 51849 | 02.92 | County School | UR |
| 51887 | 08.92 | West Somerset Railway | |

CLASS 108 — DMBS

Built: 1960-61 by BR at Derby C & W Works.
Engines: Two horizontal Leyland 680/1 or 680/13 type of 112 kW at 1800 rpm.
Transmission: Mechanical.
Length over buffers: 18.491 m.   **Weight:** 29.05 t.
Extreme width: 2.819 m.   **Seats:** 52.
Extreme height: 3.874 m.   **Toilet:** Not equipped.
Maximum Permitted Speed: 70 mph.

51907	02.93	Llangollen Railway	OP
51919	02.93	Bodmin & Wenford Railway	
51922	06.92	National Railway Museum	UR
51933	02.93	Peak Rail PLC	
51935	10.92	Severn Valley Railway	
51941	11.90	Severn Valley Railway	OP
51947	02.93	Bodmin & Wenford Railway	
51950	06.91	Gloucestershire Warwickshire Railway	OP

CLASS 107 DMBS

Built: 1961 by BR at Derby C & W Works.
Engines: Two horizontal Leyland 1595 type of 112 kW at 1800 rpm.
Transmission: Mechanical.
Length over buffers: 18.491 m.   **Weight:** 34.45 t.
Extreme width: 2.819 m.   **Seats:** 52.
Extreme height: 3.874 m.   **Toilet:** Not equipped.
Maximum Permitted Speed: 70 mph.

| 52006 | 10.92 | East Kent Light Railway | OP |
| 52008 | 10.92 | | SB |

CLASS 107 DMCL

Built: 1961 by BR at Derby C & W Works.
Engines: Two horizontal Leyland 1595 type of 112 kW at 1800 rpm.
Transmission: Mechanical.
Length over buffers: 18.491 m.   **Weight:** 34.45 t.
Extreme width: 2.819 m.   **Seats:** 12 1st, 53 2nd.
Extreme height: 3.874 m.   **Toilet:** 1.
Maximum Permitted Speed: 70 mph.

| 52029 | 10.92 | Lakeside & Haverthwaite Railway | |
| 52031 | 10.92 | East Kent Light Railway | OP |

CLASS 108 DMCL

Built: 1960-61 by BR at Derby C & W Works.
Engines: Two horizontal Leyland 680/1 type of 112 kW at 1800 rpm.
Transmission: Mechanical.
Length over buffers: 18.491 m.   **Weight:** 28.05 t.
Extreme width: 2.794 m.   **Seats:** 12 1st, 50 2nd.
Extreme height: 3.874 m.   **Toilet:** 1.
Maximum Permitted Speed: 70 mph.

52044	02.93		SB
52048	02.93	Bodmin & Wenford Railway	
52054	02.93	Bodmin & Wenford Railway	
52062	06.91	Gloucestershire Warwickshire Railway	UR
52064	11.90	Severn Valley Railway	OP

CLASS 110   DMBC

Built: 1962 by Birmingham Railway Carriage & Wagon Company, Smethwick.
Engines: Two Rolls Royce C6NFLH138D type of 134 kW at 1800 rpm.
Transmission: Mechanical.
Length over buffers: 18.485 m.   **Weight:** 32.00 t.
Extreme width: 2.819 m.   **Seats:** 12 1st, 33 2nd.
Extreme height: 3.835 m.   **Toilet:** Not equipped.
Maximum Permitted Speed: 70 mph.

| 52071 | 03.90 | Lakeside & Haverthwaite Railway | OP |

CLASS 110   DMCL

Built: 1961 by Birmingham Railway Carriage & Wagon Company, Smethwick.
Engines: Two Rolls Royce C6NFLH138D type of 134 kW at 1800 rpm.
Transmission: Mechanical.
Length over buffers: 18.485 m.   **Weight:** 32.00 t.
Extreme width: 2.819 m.   **Seats:** 12 1st, 54 2nd.
Extreme height: 3.835 m.   **Toilet:** 1.
Maximum Permitted Speed: 70 mph.

| 52077 | 03.90 | Lakeside & Haverthwaite Railway | OP |

CLASS 114   DMBS

Built: 1956 by BR at Derby C & W Works.
Engines: Two horizontal Leyland type 680/1 of 112 kW at 1800 rpm.
Transmission: Mechanical.
Length over buffers: 20.447 m.   **Weight:** 37.50 t.
Extreme width: 2.819 m.   **Seats:** 62.
Extreme height: 3.861 m.   **Toilet:** Not equipped.
Maximum Permitted Speed: 70 mph.

| 53019 | 50019 | 06.92 | Midland Railway Centre | OP |

CLASS 104   DMBS

Built: 1957-58 by Birmingham Railway Carriage & Wagon Company, Smethwick.
Engines: Two horizontal Leyland 680/1 type of 112 kW (150 hp).

Transmission: Mechanical.

Length over buffers: 18.491 m.	**Weight:** 31.00 t.
Extreme width: 2.819 m.	**Seats:** 52.
Extreme height: 3.835 m.	**Toilet:** Not equipped.

Maximum Permitted Speed: 70 mph.

53437	50437	02.92		SB
53447	50447	03.92	Llangollen Railway (For Spares)	SU
53454	50454	03.92	Llangollen Railway	OP
53455	50455	09.92		SB
53479	50479	02.92		SB

CLASS 104   DMCL

Built: 1957-58 by Birmingham Railway Carriage & Wagon Company, Smethwick.
Engines: Two horizontal Leyland 680/1 type of 112 kW (150 hp).
Transmission: Mechanical.

Length over buffers: 18.491 m.	**Weight:** 31.00 t.
Extreme width: 2.819 m.	**Seats:** 12 1st, 54 (* 51) 2nd.
Extreme height: 3.835 (* 3.880) m.	**Toilet:** 1.

Maximum Permitted Speed: 70 mph.

53494	50494	06.90		SB
53517	50517	05.90		SB
53528	50528	03.92	Llangollen Railway	OP
53531	50531	03.92	Cambrian Railways Society	SU
53556*	50556	05.89	Cambrian Railways Society	SU

CLASS 108   DMBS

Built: 1958 by BR at Derby C & W Works.
Engines: Two horizontal Leyland 680/1 type of 112 kW (150 hp).
Transmission: Mechanical.

Length over buffers: 18.491 m.	**Weight:** 29.05 t.
Extreme width: 2.794 m.	**Seats:** 52.
Extreme height: 3.874 m.	**Toilet:** Not equipped.

Maximum Permitted Speed: 70 mph.

| 53599 | 50599 | 01.93 | | SB |
| 53619 | 50619 | 07.91 | Dean Forest Railway | UR |

CLASS 108   DMCL

Built: 1958 by BR at Derby C & W Works.
Engines: Two horizontal Leyland 680/1 type of 112 kW at 1800 rpm.
Transmission: Mechanical.

Length over buffers: 18.491 m.
Extreme width: 2.794 m.
Extreme height: 3.874 m.
Weight: 28.05 t.
Seats: 12 1st, 50 2nd.
Toilet: 1.
Maximum Permitted Speed: 70 mph.

53632	50632	02.93		SB
53645	50645	02.93	Bodmin & Wenford Railway	

CLASS 108 — DMBS

Built: 1959-60 by BR at Derby C & W Works.
Engines: Two horizontal Leyland 680/1 type of 112 kW (150 hp).
Transmission: Mechanical.
Length over buffers: 18.491 m.
Extreme width: 2.794 m.
Extreme height: 3.874 m.
Weight: 29.05 t.
Seats: 52.
Toilet: Not equipped.
Maximum Permitted Speed: 70 mph.

53928	50928	03.92	Keighley & Worth Valley Railway	OP
53933	50933	11.92	Peak Rail PLC	UR
53971	50971			SB
53980	50980	02.93	Bodmin & Wenford Railway	

CLASS 114 — DTCL

Built: 1956-57 by BR at Derby C & W Works.
Length over buffers: 20.447 m.
Extreme width: 2.819 m.
Extreme height: 3.874 m.
Weight: 29.55 t.
Seats: 12 1st, 62 2nd.
Toilet: 1.
Maximum Permitted Speed: 70 mph.

54006	56006	03.92	Midland Railway Centre	OP
54047	56047	10.91		SB

CLASS 108 — DTCL

Built: 1958-60 by BR at Derby C & W Works.
Length over buffers: 18.491 m.
Extreme width: 2.737 m.
Extreme height: 3.874 m.
Weight: 21.15 t.
Seats: 12 1st, 53 2nd.
Toilet: 1.
Maximum Permitted Speed: 70 mph.

54207	56207	07.90	British Steel, Scunthorpe	OH
54224	56224	09.92	East Kent Light Railway	
54274	56274	02.92	Rutland Railway Museum	UR

CLASS 121 DTS

Built: 1961 by Pressed Steel, Linwood.
Length over buffers: 20.447 m.   **Weight:** 29.35 t.
Extreme width: 2.819 m.   **Seats:** 91.
Extreme height: 3.861 m.   **Toilet:** Not equipped.
Maximum Permitted Speed: 70 mph.

54287	56287	04.92	Battlefield Steam Railway	
54289	56289	12.92	Mangapps Farm Railway Museum	

CLASS 105 DTCL

Built: 1959 by Cravens, Sheffield.
Length over buffers: 18.491 m.   **Weight:** 24.10 t.
Extreme width: 2.819 m.   **Seats:** 12 1st, 51 2nd.
Extreme height: 3.772 m.   **Toilet:** 1.
Maximum Permitted Speed: 70 mph.

54456	56456	07.83	Llangollen Railway	OP

CLASS 108 DTCL

Built: 1960 by BR at Derby C & W Works.
Length over buffers: 18.491 m.   **Weight:** 21.15 t.
Extreme width: 2.794 m.   **Seats:** 12 1st, 53 2nd.
Extreme height: 3.874 m.   **Toilet:** 1.
Maximum Permitted Speed: 70 mph.

54484	56484	07.92	Peak Rail PLC	
54490	56490	02.93	Llangollen Railway	OP
54491	56491	12.92		SB
54492	56492	07.91	Dean Forest Railway	UR
54504	56504	02.93	Peak Rail PLC	

CLASS 122 DMBS

Built: 1958 by Gloucester Railway Carriage & Wagon Company, Gloucester.
Engines: Two horizontal AEC 220 type of 112 kW at 1800 rpm.
Transmission: Mechanical.
Length over buffers: 20.447 m.   **Weight:** 36.50 t.
Extreme width: 2.743 m.   **Seats:** 65.
Extreme height: 3.861 m.   **Toilet:** Not equipped
Maximum Permitted Speed: 70 mph.

55005	10.92	Battlefield Steam Railway	OP

CLASS 127   DMPMV

Built: 1959 by BR at Derby C & W Works. Converted for parcels use 1985.
Engines: Two Rolls Royce C8NFLH823 type of 178 kW at 1800 rpm.
Transmission: Hydraulic.
Length over buffers: 20.447 m.   **Weight:** 39.85 t.
Extreme width: 2.819 m.   **Carrying Capacity:** 10 t.
Extreme height: 3.874 m.   **Toilet:** Not equipped.
Maximum Permitted Speed: 70 mph.

55966	51591	05.89	Midland Railway Centre	OP
55967	51610	05.89	Swindon & Cricklade Railway	CC
55976	51625	05.89	Midland Railway Centre	OP
55986	51627	05.89	The Railway Age, Crewe	

CLASS 100   DTCL

Built: 1957 by Gloucester Railway Carriage & Wagon Company, Gloucester.
Length over buffers: 18.491 m.   **Weight:** 25.10 t.
Extreme width: 2.819 m.   **Seats:** 12 1st, 54 2nd.
Extreme height: 3.874 m.   **Toilet:** 1.
Maximum Permitted Speed: 70 mph.

56097		10.72	West Somerset Railway	SS

CLASS 105   DTCL

Built: 1957 by Cravens, Sheffield.
Length over buffers: 18.491 m.   **Weight:** 23.15 t.
Extreme width: 2.819 m.   **Seats:** 12 1st, 51 2nd.
Extreme height: 3.835 m.   **Toilet:** 1.
Maximum Permitted Speed: 70 mph.

56121		05.81	West Somerset Railway	OP

CLASS 103   DTCL

Built: 1958 by Park Royal Vehicles, London.
Length over buffers: 18.491 m.   **Weight:** 26.55 t.
Extreme width: 2.819 m.   **Seats:** 16 1st, 48 2nd.
Extreme height: 3.772 m.   **Toilet:** 1.
Maximum Permitted Speed: 70 mph.

56160		02.71	Battlefield Steam Railway	SU
56169		12.72	West Somerset Railway	SU

UNCLASSIFIED   DTCL

Built: 1957-58 by D. Wickham, Ware.
Length over buffers: 18.491 m.   **Weight:** 22.50 t.
Extreme width: 2.819 m.   **Seats:** 16 1st, 50 2nd
Extreme height: 3.835 m.   **Toilet:** 1.
Maximum Permitted Speed: 70 mph.

56170	09.61	Trinidad Government Railways	EX
56171	10.67	Llangollen Railway	UR
56174	09.61	Trinidad Government Railways	EX

CLASS 100   DTCL

Built: 1957-58 by Gloucester Railway Carriage & Wagon Company, Gloucester.
Length over buffers: 18.491 m.   **Weight:** 25.10 t.
Extreme width: 2.819 m.   **Seats:** 12 1st, 54 2nd.
Extreme height: 3.874 m.   **Toilet:** 1.
Maximum Permitted Speed: 70 mph.

56301	02.72	Uranium Fuel Centre	OH
56317	04.74	Gwili Railway/Rheilffordd Gwili	OH

CLASS 116   TC

Built: 1957 by BR at Derby C & W Works.
Length over buffers: 20.447 m.   **Weight:** 28.55 t.
Extreme width: 2.819 m.   **Seats:** 28 1st, 74 2nd.
Extreme height: 3.874 m.   **Toilet:** Not equipped.
Maximum Permitted Speed: 70 mph.

59003	11.83	South Devon Railway	OH
59004	11.83	South Devon Railway	OH

CLASS 126   TBFKL

Built: 1961 by BR at Swindon Works.
Length over buffers: 20.155 m.   **Weight:**
Extreme width: 2.819 m.   **Seats:** 18.
Extreme height: 3.886 m.   **Toilets:** 2.
Maximum Permitted Speed: 70 mph.

59098	10.72	North Yorkshire Moors Railway	CC
59099	10.72	North Yorkshire Moors Railway	CC

CLASS 104   TCL

Built: 1957 by Birmingham Railway Carriage & Wagon Company, Smethwick.
Length over buffers: 18.491 m.   **Weight:** 24.10 t.
Extreme width: 2.819 m.   **Seats:** 12 1st, 54 2nd.
Extreme height: 3.880 m.   **Toilet:** 1.
Maximum Permitted Speed: 70 mph.
59137   10.89   SB

CLASS 104   TBSL

Built: 1958 by Birmingham Railway Carriage & Wagon Company, Smethwick.
Length over buffers: 18.491 m.   **Weight:** 25.00 t.
Extreme width: 2.819 m.   **Seats:** 51.
Extreme height: 3.880 m.   **Toilet:** 1.
Maximum Permitted Speed: 70 mph.
59228   01.91   Cambrian Railways Society   SU

CLASS 108   TBSL

Built: 1958 by BR at Derby C & W Works.
Length over buffers: 18.491 m.   **Weight:** 23.15 t.
Extreme width: 2.794 m.   **Seats:** 50.
Extreme height: 3.874 m.   **Toilet:** 1.
Maximum Permitted Speed: 70 mph.
59245   07.90   British Steel, Scunthorpe   OH
59250   07.91   Severn Valley Railway   OP

CLASS 120   TSLRB

Built: 1958 BR at Swindon Works.
Length over buffers: 20.447 m.   **Weight:** 30.50 t.
Extreme width: 2.819 m.   **Seats:** 60.
Extreme height: 3.899 m.   **Toilet:** 1.
Maximum Permitted Speed: 70 mph.
59276   11.83   Great Central Railway   UR

CLASS 108   TSL

Built: 1958 by BR at Derby C & W Works.
Length over buffers: 18.491 m.   **Weight:** 23.50 t.
Extreme width: 2.794 m.   **Seats:** 68.

Extreme height: 3.874 m.   **Toilet:** 1.
Maximum Permitted Speed: 70 mph.

| 59387 | 11.92 | Peak Rail PLC | UR |

CLASS 126   TCL

Built: 1959 by BR at Swindon Works.
Length over buffers: 20.155 m.   **Weight:** 31.50 t.
Extreme width: 2.819 m.   **Seats:** 18 1st, 32 2nd.
Extreme height: 3.899 m.   **Toilets:** 2.
Maximum Permitted Speed: 70 mph.

| 59404 | 12.82 | Caledonian Railway | SU |

CLASS 116   TC

Built: 1958 by BR at Derby C & W Works.
Length over buffers: 20.447 m.   **Weight:** 28.55 t.
Extreme width: 2.819 m.   **Seats:** 28 1st, 74 2nd.
Extreme height: 3.874 m.   **Toilet:** Not equipped.
Maximum Permitted Speed: 70 mph.

| 59444 | 07.90 | Chasewater Light Railway | OH |
| 59445 | 10.92 | Allied Steel & Wire, Cardiff | UR |

CLASS 111   TSLRB

Built: 1960 by Metropolitan Cammell, Birmingham.
Length over buffers: 18.491 m.   **Weight:** 25.10 t.
Extreme width: 2.819 m.   **Seats:** 53.
Extreme height: 3.848 m.   **Toilet:** 1.
Maximum Permitted Speed: 70 mph.

| 59575 | 09.75 | Museum of Science & Industry (Manchester) | IE |

CLASS 115   TS

Built: 1960 by BR at Derby C & W Works.
Length over buffers: 20.447 m.   **Weight:** 29.05 t.
Extreme width: 2.819 m.   **Seats:** 106.
Extreme height: 3.861 m.   **Toilet:** Not equipped.
Maximum Permitted Speed: 70 mph.

| 59659 | 08.92 | South Devon Railway | |

CLASS 115   TCL

Built: 1960 by BR at Derby C & W Works.
Length over buffers: 20.447 m.   **Weight:** 30.00 t.
Extreme width: 2.819 m.   **Seats:** 30 1st, 40 2nd.
Extreme height: 3.861 m.   **Toilet:** 1.
Maximum Permitted Speed: 70 mph.

59664	08.92	County School	UR
59678	08.92	West Somerset Railway	

CLASS 110   TSL

Built: 1961 by Birmingham Railway Carriage & Wagon Company, Smethwick.
Length over buffers: 18.478 m.   **Weight:** 24.10 t.
Extreme width: 2.819 m.   **Seats:** 72.
Extreme height: 3.874 m.   **Toilet:** 1.
Maximum Permitted Speed: 70 mph.

59701	04.91	Battlefield Steam Railway	UR

CLASS 115   TCL

Built: 1960 by BR at Derby C & W Works.
Length over buffers: 20.447 m.   **Weight:** 30.00 t.
Extreme width: 2.819 m.   **Seats:** 30 1st, 40 2nd.
Extreme height: 3.861 m.   **Toilet:** 1.
Maximum Permitted Speed: 70 mph.

59719	12.90	South Devon Railway

CLASS 201   DMBS

Built: 1957 by BR at Eastleigh Works/Ashford Works.
Engine: English Electric type 4SRKT Mk.2 rated at 373 kW.
Transmission: Electric.
Length overall: 18.358 m.   **Weight:** 54.00 t.
Extreme width: 2.743 m.   **Seats:** 22.
Extreme height: 3.829 m.   **Toilet:** Not equipped.
Maximum Permitted Speed: 75 mph.

60000	09.86	Kent & East Sussex Railway	OP
60001	09.86	St. Leonards Railway Engineering	UR

CLASS 202   DMBS

Built: 1957 by BR at Eastleigh Works/Ashford Works.
Engine: English Electric type 4SRKT Mk.2 rated at 373 kW.
Transmission: Electric.
Length overall: 20.339 m.   **Weight:** 55.00 t.
Extreme width: 2.743 m.   **Seats:** 30.
Extreme height: 3.829 m.   **Toilet:** Not equipped.
Maximum Permitted Speed: 75 mph.

60016	09.86	Kent & East Sussex Railway	OP
60018	06.88	St. Leonards Railway Engineering	OP
60019	06.88	St. Leonards Railway Engineering	SU

CLASS 201   TSL

Built: 1957 by BR at Eastleigh Works/Ashford Works.
Length overall: 18.358 m.   **Weight:** 29.00 t.
Extreme width: 2.743 m.   **Seats:** 52.
Extreme height: 3.829 m.   **Toilets:** 2.
Maximum Permitted Speed: 75 mph.

60500	09.86	St. Leonards Railway Engineering	SU
60501	09.86	St. Leonards Railway Engineering	SU
60502	09.86	St. Leonards Railway Engineering	SU

CLASS 202   TSL

Built: 1957 by BR at Eastleigh Works/Ashford Works.
Length overall: 20.339 m.   **Weight:** 30.00 t.
Extreme width: 2.743 m.   **Seats:** 60.
Extreme height: 3.829 m.   **Toilets:** 2.
Maximum Permitted Speed: 75 mph.

60527	06.88	St. Leonards Railway Engineering	OP
60528	06.88	St. Leonards Railway Engineering	SU
60529	06.88	Kent & East Sussex Railway	OP

CLASS 201   TFLK

Built: 1957 by BR at Eastleigh Works/Ashford Works.
Length overall: 18.358 m.   **Weight:** 30.00 t.
Extreme width: 2.743 m.   **Seats:** 42.
Extreme height: 3.829 m.   **Toilets:** 2.
Maximum Permitted Speed: 75 mph.

60700	09.86	St. Leonards Railway Engineering	SU

CLASS 201 TFLK

Built: 1957 by BR at Eastleigh Works/Ashford Works.
Length overall: 18.358 m.   **Weight:** 31.00 t.
Extreme width: 2.743 m.   **Seats:** 48.
Extreme height: 3.829 m.   **Toilets:** 2.
Maximum Permitted Speed: 75 mph.

60708	09.86	St. Leonards Railway Engineering	UR
60709	06.88	St. Leonards Railway Engineering	SU

CLASS 201 TRB

Built: 1958 by BR at Eastleigh Works/Ashford Works.
Length overall: 18.358 m.   **Weight:** 30.00 t.
Extreme width: 2.743 m.   **Seats:** 21 unclassified.
Extreme height: 3.835 m.   **Toilet:** 1 (Staff use only).
Maximum Permitted Speed: 75 mph.

60750	01.64	St. Leonards Railway Engineering	SU

CLASS 126 DMBSL

Built: 1956-57 by BR at Swindon Works.
Engines: Two horizontal AEC 220 type of 112 kW at 1800 rpm.
Transmission: Mechanical.
Length over buffers: 20.447 m.   **Weight:** 38.85 t.
Extreme width: 2.819 m.   **Seats:** 52.
Extreme height: 3.899 m.   **Toilets:** 2.
Maximum Permitted Speed: 70 mph.

79091	10.72	LAMCO Mining Co, Liberia	EX
79093	10.72	LAMCO Mining Co, Liberia	EX
79094	10.72	LAMCO Mining Co, Liberia	EX
79096	10.72	LAMCO Mining Co, Liberia	EX
79097	10.72	LAMCO Mining Co, Liberia	EX

CLASS 126 TBFKL

Built: 1957 by BR at Swindon Works.
Length over buffers: 20.155 m.   **Weight:**
Extreme width: 2.819 m.   **Seats:** 18.
Extreme height: 3.886 m.   **Toilets:** 2.
Maximum Permitted Speed: 70 mph.

79443	10.72	North Yorkshire Moors Railway	CC

UNCLASSIFIED DMS

Built: 1958 by Waggon und Maschinenbau, Donauwörth, West Germany.
Engine: One Büssing type U10 of 112 kW at 1900 rpm.
Transmission: Mechanical.
Length over buffers: 13.950 m.   **Weight:** 15.00 t.
Extreme width: 2.648 m.   **Seats:** 56.
Extreme height: 3.607 m.   **Toilet:** Not equipped.
Maximum Permitted Speed: 55 mph.

79960	11.66	North Norfolk Railway	OP
79962	11.66	Keighley & Worth Valley Railway	SU
79963	11.66	North Norfolk Railway	OP
79964	04.67	Keighley & Worth Valley Railway	OP

UNCLASSIFIED DMS

Built: 1958 by AC Cars, Thames Ditton.
Engine: One horizontal AEC 220 type of 112 kW at 1800 rpm.
Transmission: Mechanical.
Length over buffers: 11.328 m.   **Weight:** 11.00 t.
Extreme width: 2.819 m.   **Seats:** 46.
Extreme height: 3.721 m.   **Toilet:** Not equipped.
Maximum Permitted Speed: 58 mph.

79976	02.68	Bodmin & Wenford Railway	SU
79978	02.68	Colne Valley Railway	OP

2.2 "SECOND GENERATION" VEHICLES

CLASS R1 DMS

Built: 1978 by Leyland Bus, Workington/BREL, Derby C & W Works.
Engine: One horizontal Leyland 510 type of 149 kW at 1800 rpm.
Transmission: Mechanical.
Length overall: 12.400 m.   **Weight:** 14.00 t.
Extreme width: 2.500 m.   **Seats:** 44.
Extreme height: 3.900 m.   **Toilet:** Not equipped.
Maximum Permitted Speed: 75 mph.
Note: Originally an unpowered test vehicle. Power unit fitted 05.79.

975874	LEV 1	.78	National Railway Museum	SU

(Robert Greengrass)

▲ Railbus 79664 awaits departure from Keighley on 3rd April 1993.

CLASS R3/1   DMS

Built: 1981 by D. Wickham, Ware.
Engine: One horizontal Leyland 690 type of 149 kW at 1800 rpm.
Transmission: Mechanical.

Length over body: 15.300 m.	**Weight:** 19.96 t.	
Extreme width: 2.970 m.	**Seats:** 56.	
Extreme height: 3.965 m.	**Toilet:** Not equipped.	

Maximum Permitted Speed: 75 mph.

977020 R3	??.??	Northern Ireland Railways	OP

CLASS R3/2   DMS

Built: 1981 by Leyland Bus, Workington/BREL Derby C & W Works.
Engine: One horizontal Leyland TL11 type of 149 kW at 1800 rpm.
Transmission: Mechanical.

Length over body: 15.300 m.	**Weight:** 19.40 t.	
Extreme width: 2.970 m.	**Seats:** 56.	
Extreme height: 3.965 m.	**Toilet:** Not equipped.	

Maximum Permitted Speed: 75 mph.

	.81	Steamtown, Scranton, Pennsylvania, USA.	EX

2.3 ADVANCED PASSENGER TRAIN VEHICLES

APT-E   PC

Built: 1972 by Metropolitan Cammell, Birmingham.
Power equipment: Four Leyland type 350 gas turbines, rated at 222 kW each.
Transmission: Electric.

Length overall: 23.000 m.	**Weight:** 49.00 t.	
Extreme width: 2.685 m.	**Seats:** 0.	
Extreme height: 3.640 m.	**Toilet:** Not equipped.	

Maximum Permitted Speed:

PC1	.76	National Railway Museum	CE
PC2	.76	National Railway Museum	CE

APT-E   TC

Built: 1972 by GEC Aircraft Division, Accrington.

Length overall:			Weight:	
Extreme width: 2.685 m.			Seats:	
Extreme height: 3.640 m.			Toilet:	
Maximum Permitted Speed:				
TC1	76	National Railway Museum		CE
TC2	76	National Railway Museum		CE

2.4 FORMER GREAT WESTERN RAILWAY VEHICLES

UNCLASSIFIED   DMBT

Built: 1934 by Park Royal Vehicles, London.
Engines: Two AEC Ricardo 6 cylinder of 90 kW at 2000 rpm.
Transmission: Mechanical.

Length over buffers: 19.380 m.			Weight: 26.20 t.	
Extreme width: 2.743 m.			Seats: 44.	
Extreme height: 3.556 m.			Toilets: 2.	
Maximum Permitted Speed: 70 mph.				
W4W	4	07.58	Swindon Railway Museum	CE

UNCLASSIFIED   DMBT

Built: 1940 by Great Western Railway, Swindon.
Engines: Two AEC Ricardo 6 cylinder of 78 kW at 1650 rpm.
Transmission: Mechanical.

Length over buffers: 20.015 m.			Weight: 35.65 t.	
Extreme width: 2.819 m.			Seats: 48.	
Extreme height: 3.721 m.			Toilets:	
Maximum Permitted Speed: 60 mph.				
W20W	20	10.62	Kent & East Sussex Railway	UR

UNCLASSIFIED   DMBT

Built: 1940 by Great Western Railway, Swindon.
Engines: Two AEC Ricardo 6 cylinder of 78 kW at 1650 rpm.
Transmission: Mechanical.

Length over buffers: 20.015 m.   **Weight:** 35.65 t.
Extreme width: 2.819 m.   **Seats:** 48.
Extreme height: 3.718 m.   **Toilet:** Not equipped.
Maximum Permitted Speed: 40 mph.

W22W	22	10.62	Didcot Railway Centre	OP

PART THREE - ELECTRIC MULTIPLE UNITS

3.1 POST NATIONALISATION STOCK

CLASS 370 (APT-P)   6-Car Articulated Unit

Built: 1978 by BREL, Derby Works (trailer cars) or Crewe Works (power cars).
Formation: DTS+TBF+M+TRSB+TBF+DTS.
Supply System: 25 kV ac 50Hz overhead.
Traction Motors: Four ASEA LJMA 410F body mounted per power car.
Length overall: **Weight:** 292.95 t.
Extreme width: 2.724 m.   **Seats:** 50 1st, 132 2nd.
Maximum Permitted Speed: 125 mph. **Toilets:** 5 per set.

48103	DTS	09.88	The Railway Age, Crewe	CE
48106	DTS	09.88	The Railway Age, Crewe	CE
48602	TBF	09.88	The Railway Age, Crewe	CE
48603	TBF	09.88	The Railway Age, Crewe	CE
48404	TRSB	09.88	The Railway Age, Crewe	CE
49002	M	09.88	The Railway Age, Crewe	CE
49006	M	09.88		SB

CLASS 491 (4-TC)   4-Car Trailer Unit

Built: 1966-67 (* 1974) by BR at York Works.
Formation: DTS+TBSK+TFK+DTS.
Length overall: 80.950 m.   **Weight:** 132.00 t.
Extreme width: 2.819 m.   **Seats:** 50 1st, 160 2nd.
Maximum Permitted Speed: 90 mph. **Toilets:** 3 per set.

70823	TBS	05.91	London Underground Ltd, Ruislip	OP

70824	TBS	02.92	London Underground Ltd, Ruislip	OP
70855	TFK	05.91	London Underground Ltd, Ruislip	OP
71163*	TFK	02.92	London Underground Ltd, Ruislip	OP
76297	DTS	05.91	London Underground Ltd, Ruislip	OP
76298	DTS	05.91	London Underground Ltd, Ruislip	OP
76322	DTS	02.92	London Underground Ltd, Ruislip	OP
76324	DTS	02.92	London Underground Ltd, Ruislip	OP

CLASS 485/486   Isle of Wight Stock DMBS

Built: 1931-32 by Metropolitan Cammell, Birmingham for London Electric Railway. Purchased by BR and converted in 1967 for use on the Isle of Wight.
Supply System: 630 V dc third rail.
Traction Motors: Two GEC WT54A per car.
Length overall: 16.190 m.   **Weight:** 31.75 t.
Extreme width: 2.690 m.   **Seats:** 26.
Maximum Permitted Speed: 45 mph.   **Toilet:** Not equipped.

| 2 | 11.90 | London Underground Ltd, Acton |
| 7 | 11.90 | London Underground Ltd, Acton |

CLASS 485/486   Isle of Wight Stock DTS

Built: 1925 by Metropolitan Cammell, Birmingham for London Electric Railway. Purchased by BR and converted in 1967 for use on the Isle of Wight.
Length overall: 15.820 m.   **Weight:** 17.05 t.
Extreme width: 2.690 m.   **Seats:** 38.
Maximum Permitted Speed: 45 mph.   **Toilet:** Not equipped.

| 27 | 11.90 | London Underground Ltd, Acton |

CLASS 485/486   Isle of Wight Stock TS

Built: 1924 by Cammell Laird, Birkenhead for London Electric Railway. Purchased by BR and converted in 1967 for use on the Isle of Wight.
Length overall: 15.690 m.   **Weight:** 18.95 t.
Extreme width: 2.690 m.   **Seats:** 42.
Maximum Permitted Speed: 45 mph.   **Toilet:** Not equipped.

| 44 | 11.90 | London Underground Ltd, Acton |
| 49 | 11.90 | London Underground Ltd, Acton |

CLASS 501   Watford TS

Built: 1957 by BR at Eastleigh Works.
Length: 17.42 m.   **Weight:** 29.50 t.

Extreme width: 2.819 m.   **Seats:** 92.
Maximum Permitted Speed: 60 mph. **Toilet:** Not equipped.
70170   10.85   MOD Marchwood Port Railway   OH

CLASS 501   Watford DTBS

Built: 1957 by BR at Eastleigh Works.
Length: 17.52 m.   **Weight:** 30.50 t.
Extreme width: 2.819 m.   **Seats:** 74.
Maximum Permitted Speed: 60 mph. **Toilet:** Not equipped
75186   10.85   MOD Marchwood Port Railway   OH

CLASS 504   Bury 2-Car Unit

Built: 1959 by BR at Wolverton Works.
Formation: DMBS+DTS.
Supply System: 1200 V dc third rail side contact.
Traction Motors: Four English Electric.
Length: 20.31 + 20.31 m.   **Weight:** 82.00 t.
Extreme width: 2.819 m.   **Seats:** 178.
Maximum Permitted Speed: 65 mph. **Toilet:** Not equipped.
65451   DMBS   08.91   East Lancashire Railway   OH
65461   DMBS   08.91   East Lancashire Railway   OH
77172   DTS   08.91   East Lancashire Railway   OH
77182   DTS   08.91   East Lancashire Railway   OH

CLASS 506   Hadfield 3-Car Unit

Built: 1950 by Metropolitan Cammell, Birmingham
    (* Birmingham Railway Carriage & Wagon Company, Smethwick).
Formation: DMBS+TS+DTS.
Supply System: 1500 V dc overhead.
Traction Motors: Four GEC.
Length: 18.41 + 16.78 + 16.87 m. **Weight:** 106.00 t.
Extreme width: 2.819 m.   **Seats:** 174.
Maximum Permitted Speed: 70 mph. **Toilet:** Not equipped.
59404   DMBS   12.84   Midland Railway Centre   CE
59504* TS   12.84   Midland Railway Centre   CE
59604   DTS   12.84   Midland Railway Centre   CE

UNCLASSIFIED 4-DD DMBS

Built: 1949 by BR at Lancing Works.
Supply System: 750 V dc third rail.
Traction Motors: Two English Electric.
Length over body: 19.050 m. **Weight:** 39.00 t.
Extreme width: 2.819 m. **Seats:** 120.
Maximum Permitted Speed: 75 mph. **Toilet:** Not equipped.

13003	10.71	Hope Farm	SU
13004	10.71	Northampton & Lamport Railway	UR

UNCLASSIFIED DMBS

Built: 1958 by BR at Derby/Cowlairs Works.
Supply System: 216 lead acid batteries of 1070 Ah capacity.
Traction Motors: Two Siemens-Schuckert.
Length overall: 18.491 m. **Weight:** 37.50 t.
Extreme width: 2.794 m. **Seats:** 52.
Maximum Permitted Speed: 70 mph. **Toilet:** Not equipped.

79998	12.66	East Lancashire Railway	OP

UNCLASSIFIED DTCL

Built: 1958 by BR at Derby/Cowlairs Works.
Length overall: 18.491 m. **Weight:** 37.50 t.
Extreme width: 2.794 m. **Seats:** 12 1st, 53 2nd.
Maximum Permitted Speed: 70 mph. **Toilet:** 1.

79999	12.66	East Lancashire Railway	OP

3.2 FORMER LMS & CONSTITUENT COMPANIES STOCK

CLASS 502 Southport 2-Car Unit

Built: 1939 by London Midland & Scottish Railway, Derby C & W Works
Formation: DMBS+DTS.
Supply System: 630 V dc third rail.
Traction Motors: Four English Electric.
Length: 20.26 + 20.26 m. **Weight:** 68.00 t.

Extreme width: 2.900 m. **Seats:** 167.
Maximum Permitted Speed: 65 mph. **Toilet:** Not equipped.

| 28361 | DMBS | 08.80 | Southport Railway Centre | SS |
| 29896 | DTS | 08.80 | Southport Railway Centre | SS |

CLASS 503   Wirral 3-Car Unit

Built: 1938 by Metropolitan Cammell, Birmingham (* Birmingham Railway Carriage & Wagon Company, Smethwick).
Formation: DMBS+TS+DTS.
Supply System: 650 V dc third rail.
Traction Motors: Four BTH.
Length: 17.68 + 17.07 + 17.68 m. **Weight:** 78.00 t.
Extreme width: 2.77 m. **Seats:** 176.
Maximum Permitted Speed: 65 mph. **Toilet:** Not equipped.

28690*	DMBS	03.85	Shore Road Museum, Birkenhead	CE
29289	DTS	03.85	Shore Road Museum, Birkenhead	CE
29720	TS	03.85	Shore Road Museum, Birkenhead	CE

UNCLASSIFIED   Altrincham TC

Built: 1931 by Metropolitan Cammell, Birmingham.
Length over body: 17.399 m **Weight:** 30.00 t.
Extreme width: 2.819 m. **Seats:** 24 1st, 72 2nd.
Maximum Permitted Speed: mph. **Toilet:** Not equipped.

29663	05.71	Midland Railway Centre	CE
29666	05.71	Midland Railway Centre	CE
29670	05.71	Midland Railway Centre	CE

UNCLASSIFIED   Watford DMBS

Built: 1915 by Metropolitan Cammell, Birmingham.
Supply System: 630 V dc third rail.
Traction Motors: Four Oerlikon.
Length over body: 17.600 m. **Weight:** 54.75 t.
Extreme width: 2.73 m. **Seats:** 48.
Maximum Permitted Speed: mph. **Toilet:** Not equipped.

| 28249 | 05.62 | National Railway Museum | CE |

CLASS 487   Waterloo & City DMBS

Built: 1940 by English Electric, Preston.
Supply System: 630 V dc third rail.
Traction Motors: Two English Electric 500.
Length overall: 14.860 m.   **Weight:** 29.00 t.
Extreme width: 2.640 m.   **Seats:** 40.
Maximum Permitted Speed: 35 mph.   **Toilet:** Not equipped.

| 61 | 05.93 | National Railway Museum | OP |

1285 CLASS   3-Sub DMBS

Built: 1925 by Metropolitan Cammell, Birmingham.
Supply System: 750 V dc third rail.
Traction Motors: Two Metropolitan Vickers.
Length overall: **Weight:**
Extreme width: **Seats:**
Maximum Permitted Speed: 75 mph.   **Toilet:** Not equipped.

| 8143 | 11.60 | National Railway Museum | CE |

UNCLASSIFIED   4-Cor TSK

Built: 1938 by Southern Railway, Eastleigh Works.
Length over body: 19.355 m.   **Weight:** 32.65 t.
Extreme width: 2.819 m.   **Seats:** 68.
Maximum Permitted Speed: 75 mph.   **Toilet:** 1.

| 10096 | 12.72 | St. Leonards Railway Engineering | UR |

UNCLASSIFIED   2-Bil DTCL

Built: 1937 by Southern Railway, Eastleigh Works.
Length over body: 19.050 m.   **Weight:** 31.25 t.
Extreme width: 2.819 m.   **Seats:** 24 1st, 32 2nd.
Maximum Permitted Speed: 75 mph.   **Toilet:** 1

| 10656 | 08.71 | BR Brighton Depot | ML |

UNCLASSIFIED   4-Res DMBS

Built: 1937 by Southern Railway, Eastleigh Works.
Supply System: 750 V dc third rail.
Traction Motors: Two English Electric.
Length over body: 19.355 m.   **Weight:** 46.50 t.
Extreme width: 2.858 m.   **Seats:** 52.
Maximum Permitted Speed: 75 mph. **Toilet:** Not equipped.

11161	09.72	St. Leonards Railway Engineering	UR

UNCLASSIFIED   4-Cor DMBS

Built: 1937-38 by Southern Railway, Eastleigh Works.
Supply System: 750 V dc third rail.
Traction Motors: Two English Electric.
Length over body: 19.355 m.   **Weight:** 46.50 t.
Extreme width: 2.858 m.   **Seats:** 52.
Maximum Permitted Speed: 75 mph. **Toilet:** Not equipped.

11179	09.72	National Railway Museum	CE
11187	09.72	Swanage Railway	SU
11201	09.72	St. Leonards Railway Engineering	UR

UNCLASSIFIED   6-Pul TCK

Built: 1932 by Southern Railway, Eastleigh Works.
Length over body: 19.355 m.   **Weight:** 32.60 t.
Extreme width: 2.819 m.   **Seats:** 30 1st, 24 2nd.
Maximum Permitted Speed: 75 mph. **Toilet:** 1.

11773	.72	Swanage Railway

UNCLASSIFIED   4-Cor TCK

Built: 1937 by Southern Railway, Eastleigh Works.
Length over body: 19.355 m.   **Weight:** 32.60 t.
Extreme width: 2.819 m.   **Seats:** 30 1st, 24 2nd.
Maximum Permitted Speed: 75 mph. **Toilet:** 1.

11825	.72	St. Leonards Railway Engineering

UNCLASSIFIED   2-Bil DMBSL

Built: 1937 by Southern Railway, Eastleigh Works.
Supply System: 750 V dc third rail.

Traction Motors: Two English Electric.
Length over body: 19.050 m.   **Weight:** 43.50 t.
Extreme width: 2.819 m.   **Seats:** 52.
Maximum Permitted Speed: 75 mph.   **Toilet:** 1.

12123	08.71	BR Brighton Depot	ML

3.4 FORMER LNER & CONSTITUENT COMPANIES STOCK

GRIMSBY & IMMINGHAM LIGHT RAILWAY TRAM

Built: 1914 by Great Central Railway, Dukinfield Works.
Supply System:
Traction Motors: Two Dick Kerr.
Length over body: **Weight:**
Extreme width: **Seats:** 64.
Maximum Permitted Speed: **Toilet:** Not equipped.

14	07.61	National Tramway Museum

GRIMSBY & IMMINGHAM LIGHT RAILWAY TRAMS

Built: 1925-7 by Gateshead & District Tramways Company, Gateshead.
Supply System:
Traction Motors:
Length over body: **Weight:**
Extreme width: **Seats:** 48.
Maximum Permitted Speed: **Toilet:** Not equipped.

20	07.61	National Tramway Museum	
26	07.61	Beamish	OP

UNCLASSIFIED   North Tyneside DMPV

Built: 1904 by North Eastern Railway, York Works.
Supply System: 675 V dc third rail.
Traction Motors:
Length over body: 17.400 m.   **Weight:** 46.00 t.
Extreme width: 2.772 m.   **Seats:** Not equipped.
Maximum Permitted Speed: **Toilet:** Not equipped.

900730	.38	North Tyneside Steam Railway	CE

3.5 FORMER PULLMAN COMPANY STOCK

UNCLASSIFIED   6-Pul TPCK

Built: 1932 by Metropolitan Cammell, Birmingham.
Length over body: 20.400 m.   **Weight:** 43.00 t.
Extreme width: 2.772 m.   **Seats:**
Maximum Permitted Speed: 75 mph. **Toilet:**

| 264 | Ruth | 09.65 | VSOE at BR Stewarts Lane Depot | UR |
| 278 | Bertha | 06.66 | Bluebell Railway | OH |

UNCLASSIFIED   5-Bel TPKF

Built: 1932 by Metropolitan Cammell, Birmingham.
Length over body: 20.117 m.   **Weight:** 43.00 t.
Extreme width: 2.731 m.   **Seats:** 20.
Maximum Permitted Speed: 75 mph. **Toilet:**

279	Hazel	04.72	The Black Bull, Moulton	CE
280	Audrey	04.72	VSOE (at BR Stewarts Lane Depot)	ML
281	Gwen	04.72	VSOE (at BR Stewarts Lane Depot)	
282	Doris	04.72	CIL Shopfitters, Finsbury Park	CE
283	Mona	04.72	The Brighton Belle, Winsford	CE
284	Vera	04.72	VSOE (at BR Stewarts Lane Depot)	ML

UNCLASSIFIED   5-Bel TPS

Built: 1932 by Metropolitan Cammell, Birmingham.
Length over body: 20.117 m.   **Weight:** 39.00 t.
Extreme width: 2.731 m.   **Seats:** 56.
Maximum Permitted Speed: 75 mph. **Toilet:**

85		04.72	The Nags Head, Mickleover	CE
86		04.72	VSOE (at BR Stewarts Lane Depot)	
87		04.72	North Norfolk Railway	OH

UNCLASSIFIED   5-Bel DMPBS

Built: 1932 by Metropolitan Cammell, Birmingham.
Supply System: 750 V dc third rail.
Traction Motors: Four BTH.
Length over body: 20.117 m.   **Weight:** 62.00 t.

Extreme width: 2.731 m. **Seats:** 48.
Maximum Permitted Speed: 75 mph. **Toilet:**

88	04.72	VSOE (at BR Stewarts Lane Depot)	
89	04.72	Little Mill Inn, Rowarth	CE
90	04.72	East Lancashire Railway	SU
91	04.72	North Norfolk Railway	OH
92	04.72	Brighton Railway Museum	SU
93	04.72	Brighton Railway Museum	SU

LOCOMOTIVE NAMES

Names are listed in the same order as the vehicles are listed. Names bestowed since acquisition from BR are shown in italic typeface.

02003	*Peter*
D2867	*Diane*
D2868	*Sam*
D2023	*Faith*
03059	*Edward*
03119	*Linda*
03144	*Western Waggoner*
03162	Birkenhead South 1879-1985
D2192	*Ardent*
D2272	*Alfie*
D2578	*Cider Queen*
07011	*Cleveland*
D3002	*Dulcote*
08011	*Haversham*
D3019	*Gwyneth*
08022	*Lion*
08032	*Mendip*
08046	*Brechin City*
08060	*Unicorn*
08077	*James*
08123	*George Mason*
08164	*Prudence*
08320	*Susan*
08331	*Terence*
08398	*Annabel*
08678	*Ulverstonian*
08764	*Florence*
08774	*Arthur Vernon Dawson*

08785	*Clarence*
D3489	*Colonel Tomline*
D4067	*Margaret Ethel-Thomas Alfred Naylor*
D4092	*Christine*
20041	*Nancy*
20060	*Lorna*
20083	*Alison*
20101	*Janis*
20219	*Kilmarnock 400*
20225	*Iona*
24032	*Helen Turner*
24061	Experiment
25035	*Castel Dinas Bram*
25173	*John F. Kennedy*
25185	*Mercury*
25191	*The Diana*
25265	*Harlech Castle/Castell Harlech*
25278	*Sybillia*
25322	Tamworth Castle
33056	The Burma Star
33111	Templecombe
D7017	*Williton*
40012	Aureol
40013	Andania
40106	*Atlantic Conveyor*
D821	Greyhound
D832	Onslaught
44004	Great Gable
44008	Penyghent
45060	Sherwood Forester
45112	The Royal Army Ordnance Corps
45118	The Royal Artilleryman
45135	3rd Carabinier
46035	Ixion
47401	North Eastern (12.81 to 05.88). Star of the East (05.91 to 06.92)
47402	Gateshead
47403	The Geordie
50002	Superb
50008	Thunderer
50015	Valiant
50017	Royal Oak
50019	Ramilles
50021	Rodney
50026	Indomitable
50027	Lion
50031	Hood

50035	Ark Royal
50042	Triumph
50043	Eagle
50044	Exeter
50049	Defiance
D1010	Western Campaigner
D1013	Western Ranger
D1015	Western Champion
D1023	Western Fusilier
D1041	Western Prince
D1048	Western Lady
D1062	Western Courier
55002	The King's Own Yorkshire Light Infantry
55009	Alycidon
55015	Tulyar
55016	Gordon Highlander
55019	Royal Highland Fusilier
55022	Royal Scots Grey
73003	Sir Herbert Walker
E27000	Electra
E27001	Ariadne
E27003	Diana
89001	Avocet
18000	*Elisabetta*
7050	*Rorke's Drift*
7051	*John Alcock*

LIST OF INDUSTRIAL USERS

Please note that the addresses listed below are private sites and many are not normally open to the public without prior written permission.

ABB TRANSPORTATION, CREWE.
ABB Transportation Ltd., West Street, Crewe, Cheshire.

ABB TRANSPORTATION, DERBY C & W.
ABB Transportation Ltd., Litchurch Lane, Derby, Derbyshire.

ABB TRANSPORTATION, YORK.
ABB Transportation Ltd., Holgate Road, York, North Yorkshire.

ALLIED STEEL & WIRE, CARDIFF.
Allied Steel & Wire Ltd., Tremorfa Works, Cardiff, South Glamorgan.

BUTTERLEY ENGINEERING CO.
Butterley Co. Ltd, Ripley, Derbyshire.

BCOE, OXCROFT DISPOSAL POINT.
British Coal Opencast Executive, Stanfree, near Clowne, Derbyshire.

BIRDS COMMERCIAL METALS.
Birds Commercial Metals Ltd., Long Marston, Hereford & Worcester.

BLUE CIRCLE, HAMWORTHY.
Blue Circle Industries plc, Hamworthy Depot, Hamworthy, Dorset.

BRITISH COAL, WEST DRAYTON.
British Coal, West Drayton Coal Depot, Greater London.

BRITISH SALT, MIDDLEWICH.
British Salt, Cledford Lane, Middlewich, Cheshire.

BRML, EASTLEIGH.
British Rail Maintenance Limited, Campbell Road, Eastleigh, Hampshire.

CARBIBONI, COLICO, ITALY.
Carbiboni PW Contractors, Colico, Italy.

CIL SHOPFITTERS, FINSBURY PARK.
CIL Shopfitters, Finsbury Park, Greater London.

COURTAULDS, BRIDGWATER.
Courtaulds Ltd., Packaging Films, Bridgwater, Somerset.

CFD, AUTUN, FRANCE.
CFD Industrie, Autun Depot, Autun, France.

COBRA, MIDDLESBROUGH.
Cobra Railfreight Ltd., North Road, Middlesborough, Cleveland.

COBRA, WAKEFIELD.
Cobra Railfreight Ltd., Calder Vale Road, Wakefield, West Yorkshire

COSTAIN DOW-MAC, LENWADE.
Costain Dow-Mac Ltd., Atlas Works, Lenwade, Norfolk

CTTG.
Channel Tunnel Trackwork Group, Montcocol, Coquelles, France/Cheriton, Folkestone, Kent.

A.V. DAWSON, MIDDLESBROUGH.
A.V. Dawson Ltd., Depot Road, Middlesborough, Cleveland.

DAY & SON, BRENTFORD.
Day & Son, Brentford Town Goods, Brentford, Greater London.

DEANSIDE TRANSIT, GLASGOW.
Deanside Transit Ltd., Deanside Road, Hillington, Glasgow, Strathclyde.

J.M. DEMULDER, SHILTON.
J.M. DeMulder Ltd., Gun Range Farm, Shilton Lane, Shilton, near Coventry, Warwickshire.

DOW CHEMICALS, KING'S LYNN.
Dow Chemical Co. Ltd., Crossbank Road, Kings Lynn, Norfolk

ENGLISH CHINA CLAYS, FOWEY.
English China Clays Ltd., Fowey, Cornwall.

ENGLISH CHINA CLAYS, ROCKS DRIERS.
English China Clays Ltd., Goonbarrow, Bugle, Cornwall

FELIXSTOWE DOCK & RAILWAY COMPANY.
Felixstowe Dock & Railway Compnay, Felixstowe, Suffolk.

FERROUS FRAGMENTISERS, WILLESDEN.
600 Ferrous Fragmentisers Ltd., Scrubs Lane, Willesden, Greater London.

FIRE SERVICES TRAINING CENTRE, MORETON IN MARSH.
The Fire Service College. Moreton in Marsh, Gloucestershire.

FLIXBOROUGH WHARF, FLIXBOROUGH.
Flixborough Wharf Ltd., Flixborough, Scunthorpe, Humberside.

FORD MOTOR COMPANY, DAGENHAM.
Ford Motor Compnay Ltd., Dagenham, Greater London.

FOSTER YEOMAN, MEREHEAD.
Foster Yeoman Quarries Ltd., Torr Works, Shepton Mallet, Somerset.

FOSTER YEOMAN, ISLE OF GRAIN.
Foster Yeoman Quarries Ltd., Isle of Grain Site, Rochester, Kent.

FSAS, AREZZO, ITALY.
FSAS, Arezzo, Italy.

GLAXOCHEM, ULVERSTON.
Glaxochem Ltd., Ulverston, Cumbria

GULF OIL, WATERSTON.
Gulf Oil Refining Ltd., Waterston, near Milford Haven, Dyfed.

ARTHUR GUINNESS, PARK ROYAL.
Arthur Guinness, Son & Co (Park Royal) Ltd., Park Royal Brewery, Greater London.

HUMBERSIDE SEA & LAND SERVICES, GRIMSBY.
Humberside Sea & Land Services Ltd., Royal Dock, Grimsby, Humberside.

HUNSLET-BARCLAY LTD.
Hunslet-Barclay Ltd., Caledonia Works, West Longlands Street, Kilmarnock, Strathclyde.

ICI
Imperial Chemical Industries, Wilton Works, Middlesbrough, Cleveland.

INDEPENDANT SEA TERMINALS, SWALE
Independent Sea Terminals, Ridham Dock, Swale, Kent.

ISA OSPITALETTO, BRESCIA, ITALY.
ISA Ospitaletto, Brescia, Italy.

LANCASTRIAN CARRIAGE & WAGON CO, HEYSHAM.
Lancastrian Carriage & Wagon Co, Unit 2C, Port of Heysham, Industrial Bay Close, Heysham, Lancashire.

LCP FUELS, BRIERLEY HILL.
LCP Fuel Co, Pensnett Trading Estate, Shutt End, Brierley Hill, West Midlands

LINCOLN ENTERPRISE AGENCY, LINCOLN.
Lincoln Enterprise Agency, Holmes Yard, Lincoln, Lincolnshire.

LONDON UNDERGROUND LTD, ACTON.
London Underground Ltd., Acton Works, Bollo Lane, Acton, Greater London.

LONDON UNDERGROUND LTD, RUISLIP.
London Underground Ltd., West Ruislip Depot, Ruislip, Greater London

MAYER PARRY, SNAILWELL.
Mayer Parry Ltd., Snailwell, near Newmarket, Cambridgeshire

MOD, LONG MARSTON.
Ministry of Defence, Engineer Resources, Long Marston, Warwickshire.

MOD, LUDGERSHALL.
Ministry of Defence, Central Vehicle Depot, Ludgershall, Wiltshire.

MOD, MARCHWOOD.
Ministry of Defence, Marchwood Military Port, Hampshire.

OTIS EURO TRANSRAIL, SALFORD.
Otis Euro Transrail Ltd., Liverpool Road, Salford, Greater Manchester.

PD FUELS, COED BACH DP.
Powell Duffryn Coal Preparation Ltd., Coed Bach Disposal Point, Kidwelly, Dyfed.

PD FUELS, GWAUN-CAE-GURWEN DP.
Powell Duffryn Coal Preparation Ltd., Gwaun-Cae-Gurwen Disposal Point, Gwaun-Cae-Gurwen, West Glamorgan.

POTTER GROUP, ELY.
Potter Group, Queen Adelaide, Ely, Cambridgeshire.

REDLAND ROADSTONE, BARROW ON SOAR.
Redland Aggregates Ltd., Barrow on Soar, Leicestershire.

RFS KILNHURST.
RFS Locomotives Ltd., Vanguard Works, Hooton Road, Kilnhurst, South Yorkshire.

RFS DONCASTER.
RFS Engineering Ltd., Hexthorpe Road, Doncaster, South Yorkshire.

SHEERNESS STEEL CO, SHEERNESS.
Sheerness Steel Co, Sheerness, Kent.

SIDERURGICA MONTIRONE, BRESCIA, ITALY.
Siderurgica Montirone, Brescia, Italy.

SOUTHERN DEPOT COMPANY, TOLWORTH.
Southern Depot Co Ltd., Tolworth Aggregates Depot, Tolworth, Greater London.

TILCON, GRASSINGTON.
Tilcon Ltd., Swinden Lime Works, Grassington, near Skipton, North Yorkshire.

TRAFFORD PARK ESTATES, MANCHESTER.
Trafford Park Estates Co, Third Avenue, Trafford Park, Manchester, Gtr. Manchester

UIC ORE TESTING STATION.
UIC, Vienna Arsenal, Vienna, Austria.

LIST OF PRESERVATION SITES

Please note that whilst the majority of sites shown below are open to the public, days/hours of opening may be restricted and potential visitors are advised to telephone in advance for details.

BATTLEFIELD STEAM RAILWAY
Shackerstone Station, near Market Bosworth, Leicestershire. (0827-880754)

BEAMISH
The North of England Open Air Museum, Beamish, Co. Durham, DH9 0RG. (0207-231811)

BIRMINGHAM RAILWAY MUSEUM
670 Warwick Road, Tyseley Depot, Birmingham, West Midlands, B11 2HL. (021-707-4696)

BLACK BULL, THE
Moulton, Near Richmond, North Yorkshire. DL10 6QS (0325 377289)

BODMIN & WENFORD RAILWAY
Bodmin General Station, Bodmin, Cornwall, PL31 1AQ. (0208-73666)

BO'NESS & KINNEIL RAILWAY
Bo'ness Station, Union Street, Bo'ness, West Lothian, EH51 0AD. (0506-822298)

BRIGHTON BELLE, THE
Middlewich Road, Winsford, Cheshire. CW17 3NQ (0606) 593292

BRIGHTON RAILWAY MUSEUM
Preston Park, Brighton, West Sussex.

BRITISH STEEL, SCUNTHORPE
Appleby-Frodingham Works, Scunthorpe, South Humberside.

BUCKINGHAMSHIRE RAILWAY CENTRE
The Railway Station, Quainton, near Aylesbury, Buckinghamshire, HP22 4BY. (029675-450)

BULMER RAILWAY CENTRE (now closed)
Whitecross Road, Hereford.

CADEBY LIGHT RAILWAY
The Old Rectory, Cadeby, Nuneaton, Warwickshire, CV13 0AS. (0455-290462)

CAERPHILLY RAILWAY SOCIETY
Harold Wilson Industrial Estate, Van Road, Caerphilly, Mid Glamorgan. (0222-461414)

CALEDONIAN RAILWAY
The Station, 2 Park Rd., Brechin, Tayside, DD9 7AF. (0345-55965 or 0674-81318)

CAMBRIAN RAILWAYS SOCIETY
Oswestry Station Yard, Oswald Road, Oswestry, Shropshire. (0691-661648)

CHASEWATER LIGHT RAILWAY
Chasewater Pleasure Park, Brownhills, West Midlands. (0543-452623)

CHEDDLETON RAILWAY CENTRE
Cheddleton Station, near Leek, Staffordshire. (0538-360522)

CHINNOR & PRINCESS RISBOROUGH RAILWAY
Private Site in Chinnor.

CHOLSEY & WALLINGFORD RAILWAY
Hithercroft Industrial Estate, Wallingford, Oxfordshire. (0491-35067)

COLNE VALLEY RAILWAY
Castle Hedingham Station, Yeldham Road, Castle Hedingham, Halsted, Essex, CO9 3DZ. (0787-61174)

COUNTY SCHOOL
County School Station, North Elmham, Dereham, Norfolk. (0362-668181)

DARLINGTON RAILWAY CENTRE & MUSEUM
North Road Station, Darlington, County Durham, DL3 6ST. (0325-460532)

DEAN FOREST RAILWAY
Norchard Steam Centre, Lydney, Gloucestershire. (0594-845840 or 0452-840625)

EAST ANGLIAN RAILWAY MUSEUM
Chappel & Wakes Colne Station, near Colchester, Essex, CO6 2DS. (0206-242524)

EAST KENT LIGHT RAILWAY
Shepherdswell (EKLR) Station, Shepherdswell, near Dover, Kent.

EAST LANCASHIRE RAILWAY
Bolton Street Station, Bury, Greater Manchester, BL9 0EY. (061-764-7790)

EMBSAY STEAM RAILWAY
Embsay Station, Embsay, Skipton, North Yorkshire, BD23 6QX. (0756-794727)

FAWLEY HILL RAILWAY
Private Site near Henley on Thames.

GLOUCESTERSHIRE WARWICKSHIRE RAILWAY
The Station, Toddington, Cheltenham, Gloucestershire, GL54 5DT. (0242-621405)

GREAT CENTRAL RAILWAY
Central Station, Great Central Road, Loughborough, Leicestershire, LE11 1RW. (0509-230726)

GWILI RAILWAY/RHEILFFORDD GWILI
Bronwydd Arms Station, Bronwydd Arms, Carmarthen, Dyfed. (0267-230666)

HERITAGE & MARITIME MUSEUM
Old Custom House, Milford Dock, Milford Haven, Dyfed. (0646 690866)

HOPE FARM
Private Site in Kent.

HUMBERSIDE LOCOMOTIVE PRESERVATION GROUP
Dairycoates Depot, Hull, Humberside. (Site to be re-located shortly).

IRCHESTER NARROW GAUGE RAILWAY MUSEUM
Irchester Country Park, Irchester, Northamptonshire.

ISLE OF WIGHT STEAM RAILWAY
Haven Street Station, Ryde, Isle of Wight, PO33 4DS. (0983-882204)

KEIGHLEY & WORTH VALLEY RAILWAY
Haworth Station, Keighley, West Yorkshire, BD22 8NJ. (0535-645214)

KENT & EAST SUSSEX STEAM RAILWAY
Tenterden Town Station, Tenterden, Kent, TN30 6HE. (05806-5155)

LAKESIDE & HAVERTHWAITE RAILWAY
Haverthwaite Station, near Ulverston, Cumbria, LA12 8AL. (05395-31594)

LAVENDER LINE
Isfield Station, Isfield, near Uckfield, East Sussex, TN22 5XB. (0825-750515)

LINCOLN CENTRAL STATION
St. Mary Street, Lincoln, Lincolnshire.

LITTLE MILL INN
Rowarth, Derbyshire.

LLANGOLLEN RAILWAY
Llangollen Station, Abbey Road, Llangollen, Clwyd, LL20 8SN. (0978-860979)

MANGAPPS FARM
Southminster Road, Burnham-on-Crouch, Essex, CM0 8QQ. (0621-784898)

MIDDLETON RAILWAY
Moor Road, Hunslet, Leeds, West Yorkshire, LS10 2JQ.
(0532-731020 or 0532-711089)

MID-HANTS RAILWAY
Alresford Station, Alresford, Hampshire, SO24 9JG. (0962-733810/734200)

MIDLAND RAILWAY CENTRE
Butterley Station, near Ripley, Derbyshire, DE5 3TL. (0773-747674/570140)

MUSEUM OF ARMY TRANSPORT
Flemingate, Beverley, North Humberside, HU17 0NG. (0482-860445)

MUSEUM OF SCIENCE & INDUSTRY, MANCHESTER
Liverpool Road Station, Castlefield, Manchester, Greater Manchester, M3 4JP.
(061-832-2244)

NAGS HEAD, THE
Mickleover, Derbyshire. (Closed)

NARROW GAUGE RAILWAY CENTRE
Gloddfa Ganol Slate Mine, Blaenau Ffestiniog, Gwynedd, LL41 3NB. (0766830-664)

NATIONAL RAILWAY MUSEUM
Leeman Road, York, North Yorkshire, YO2 0XJ. (0904-621261)

NATIONAL TRAMWAY MUSEUM
Crich, near Matlock, Derbyshire, DE4 5DP. (0773-852565)

NENE VALLEY RAILWAY
Wansford Station, Stibbington, Peterborough, Cambridgeshire, PE8 6LR.
(0780-782845)

NORTHAMPTON & LAMPORT RAILWAY
Pitsford & Brampton Station, Pitsford, Northamptonshire. (0604-22709)

NORTH NORFOLK RAILWAY
Sheringham Station, Sheringham, Norfolk, NR26 8RA. (0263-822045)

NORTH TYNESIDE STEAM RAILWAY
Middle Engine Lane, West Chirton, North Shields, NE29 8DX. (091-262-2627)

NORTH YORKSHIRE MOORS RAILWAY
Pickering Station, Pickering, North Yorkshire. (0751-72508/73535)

PAIGHTON & DARTMOUTH STEAM RAILWAY
Queen's Park Station, Paighton, Devon. (0803-555872)

PEAK RAIL PLC
Matlock Station, Matlock, Derbyshire.

PLYM VALLEY RAILWAY
Marsh Mills Station, Coypool Road, Plymouth, Devon, PL7 4NL.

RAILWAY AGE, THE
Crewe Heritage Centre, Vernon Way, Crewe, Cheshire. (0270-212130)

ROWDEN MILL STATION MUSEUM
near Bromyard, Hereford and Worcester.

RUTLAND RAILWAY MUSEUM
Cottesmore Iron Ore Mines Siding, Ashwell Road, Cottesmore, near Oakham, Leicestershire, LE15 7BX. (0572-813203)

ST. LEONARDS RAILWAY ENGINEERING
Bridge Way, St. Leonards, East Sussex.

SCIENCE MUSEUM
Exhibition Road, South Kensington, London, SW7. (071-938-8000)

SCOTTISH INDUSTRIAL RAILWAY CENTRE
Minnivey Colliery, Dalmellington, Strathclyde. (0292-313579)

SEVERN VALLEY RAILWAY
Railway Station, Bewdley, Hereford & Worcester, DY12 1BG. (0299-403816)

SHORE ROAD MUSEUM
Shore Road Pumping Station, Hamilton Street, Birkenhead, Merseyside. (051 650 1182)

SOUTH DEVON RAILWAY
Buckfastleigh Station, Buckfastleigh, Devon. (0364-42338)

SOUTHPORT RAILWAY CENTRE
Derby Road, Southport, Merseyside, PR9 0TY. (0704-530693)

SOUTH YORKSHIRE RAILWAY
Barrow Road Railway Sidings, Barrow Road, Sheffield, S9 1LA.
(0742-424405/451214)

SPA RAILWAY
Eridge Station, Eridge Road, Eridge Green, Tunbridge Wells, Kent.

STEAMTOWN, CARNFORTH
Steamtown Railway Centre, Warton Road, Carnforth, LA5 9HX. (0524-732100)

STEAMTOWN, USA
Scranton, Pennsylvania, USA.

STOOMCENTRUM
Maldegem, Belgium

SWANAGE RAILWAY
Station House, Railway Station, Swanage, Dorset. (0929-425800)

STRATHSPEY RAILWAY
Aviemore Speyside Station, Dalfaber Road, Aviemore, Highland, PH22 1PM.
(0479-810725)

SWINDON & CRICKLADE RAILWAY
Tadpole Lane, Blunsdon, near, Swindon, Wiltshire, SN2 4DZ. (0793-771615)

TELFORD HORSEHAY STEAM TRUST
The Old Loco Shed, Horsehay, Telford, Shropshire, TF4 2LT.

URANIUM FUEL CENTRE
Springfields Factory, Salwick, Nr. Preston

UTRECHT RAILWAY MUSEUM
Utrecht, The Netherlands.

VALE OF RHEIDOL RAILWAY
Park Avenue, Aberystwyth, Dyfed, SY23 1PG. (0970-615993/625819)

VOBSTER LIGHT RAILWAY
Holwell Farm, Mells, Somerset.

WEST SOMERSET RAILWAY
The Railway Station, Minehead, Somerset. (0643-704996)

THE GROWLER GROUP

The first Class 37 rolled out of the Vulcan Foundry, Newton-le-Willows, in November 1960, carrying all over green livery and bearing the number D6701. The total number built was 309, the majority being built at Vulcan Foundry, but some were built at Robert Stephenson and Hawthorn, Darlington. The first 119 examples had split headcode identification boxes while the rest had one central headcode box. They proved their capabilities around the regions, and were equally at home on trip freights and top link expresses.

By the mid 1980s most members of the class had been in service for over 20 years and BR made a decision to give the class a life extension overhaul. This refurbishment programme began when 37268 entered Crewe Works in 1983, but was curtailed after 135 locomotives had been dealt with, when 37719 left the works in 1989.

It was during this refurbishment programme that "The Welsh Growler Group" was formed in 1986. By the time of the first AGM, interest in the Group had developed outside Wales and a decision was made to promote ourselves nationally as "THE GROWLER GROUP", with our ultimate aim to purchase and restore to full working order a Class 37 locomotive.

During 1989 the committee began looking for a home for our future acquisition, and at the end of the year we reached agreement with the Gloucestershire Warwickshire Railway, based at Toddington.

The Group has always been successful at fund raising, indeed, as well as our own tours we have worked with other organisations quite successfully, the outcome of many events leading to a profit for the Group, and enough money in the funds to buy a locomotive if a suitable example came onto the tender list. Unfortunately it is not just a matter of purchasing a locomotive, but it also has to be moved and maintained, and that's where you come in.

Membership rates for 1993 are: Junior £4, Adult £5 and Family £6. To join the Group or to find out more about us, please send a SAE to:

The Membership Secretary,

The Growler Group,

8 Gibbs Road,

NEWPORT,

Gwent, NP9 8AR.

Join now and help The Growler Group preserve and restore a Class 37.